HELPLESS
NIGHT,

*Hopeful Dawn*

*Dawn Day*

Staying Positive and Proactive
When Your Child Is Suicidal

© 2021 by Dawn Day

hopefuldawn.com

All rights reserved. In accordance with the U.S. Copyright Act of 1976, the scanning, uploading, and electronic sharing of any part of this book without permission of the publisher constitute unlawful piracy and theft of the author's intellectual property. If you would like to use material from the book (other than for review purposes), prior written permission must be obtained by contacting the author. Thank you for your support of the author's rights.

First Edition
ISBN-13: 979-8-48-579751-5

*This book is dedicated to all the angels on this earth who walked alongside my daughters and me on this journey: friends, family, and the amazing professionals who got us through.*
*We can never thank you enough.*

# TABLE OF CONTENTS

Introduction . . . . . . . . . . . . . . . . . . . . . . . . . . I
A Note from the Author . . . . . . . . . . . . . . . . . III
**PART ONE: Our Family's Journey** . . . . . . . . . . . . . . . . . . 1
    Noel . . . . . . . . . . . . . . . . . . . . . . . . . . . 3
    Desperate . . . . . . . . . . . . . . . . . . . . . . . . 9
    Blindsided . . . . . . . . . . . . . . . . . . . . . . . .13
    Alternate Reality . . . . . . . . . . . . . . . . . . . .17
    Hidden World . . . . . . . . . . . . . . . . . . . . . .23
    Despair . . . . . . . . . . . . . . . . . . . . . . . . . .27
    Evil . . . . . . . . . . . . . . . . . . . . . . . . . . . . .29
    In God's Hands . . . . . . . . . . . . . . . . . . . . .35
    Jane . . . . . . . . . . . . . . . . . . . . . . . . . . . .39
    Blame . . . . . . . . . . . . . . . . . . . . . . . . . . .43
    Crumbling . . . . . . . . . . . . . . . . . . . . . . . .45
    Digging Deep . . . . . . . . . . . . . . . . . . . . . .49
    Goodbye Letters . . . . . . . . . . . . . . . . . . . .53
    Turning Point . . . . . . . . . . . . . . . . . . . . . .59
    Rose . . . . . . . . . . . . . . . . . . . . . . . . . . . .61
    Terrified . . . . . . . . . . . . . . . . . . . . . . . . . .65
    Ready to Fly . . . . . . . . . . . . . . . . . . . . . . .71

**PART TWO: Looking Ahead** . . . . . . . . . . . . . . . . . . . . 79
    Rising Above: By Jane . . . . . . . . . . . . . . . .81
    On the Other Side: By Noel . . . . . . . . . . . .85
    Grateful: By Rose . . . . . . . . . . . . . . . . . . .89

# TABLE OF CONTENTS...CONTINUED

**PART THREE: 12 Ways to Empower Your Parenting** . . . . . 93
- 1. Find Outside Support . . . . . . . . . . . . . . . . . . 95
- 2. Let It Go. . . . . . . . . . . . . . . . . . . . . . . . . . 99
- 3. Reduce Screen Time . . . . . . . . . . . . . . . . . 105
- 4. Take Care of Yourself . . . . . . . . . . . . . . . . . 109
- 5. Avoid Unsympathetic Judgers . . . . . . . . . . 113
- 6. Surround Yourself. . . . . . . . . . . . . . . . . . . 121
- 7. Keep a Thick Skin . . . . . . . . . . . . . . . . . . . 125
- 8. Take It Day by Day . . . . . . . . . . . . . . . . . . 129
- 9. Be Gentle with Yourself . . . . . . . . . . . . . . 133
- 10. Get Real About Your Own Issues . . . . . . . . 137
- 11. Stay Positive . . . . . . . . . . . . . . . . . . . . . 141
- 12. Stay True to Unconditional Love. . . . . . . . 145

**12 Ways to Empower Your Parenting: A Reference Guide** . . 157

**PART FOUR: Helpful Resources** . . . . . . . . . . . . . . . . . . 171
- Podcast . . . . . . . . . . . . . . . . . . . . . . . . . . 172
- Books . . . . . . . . . . . . . . . . . . . . . . . . . . . 173
- Organizations . . . . . . . . . . . . . . . . . . . . . 175

**Thank You** . . . . . . . . . . . . . . . . . . . . . . . . . . . . . . 187

# INTRODUCTION

When my three daughters were born, each was such an incredible blessing. I held these beautiful babies in my arms, and like any mother, I was filled with love and hope for the future.

It's a good thing I'm not psychic.

Never in my life would I have predicted that one day, in varying degrees, all three of these precious babies would grow up to become suicidal teens.

I never would have thought that Jane, my "happy little wanderer," would one day use her writing gifts to craft goodbye letters to all those she loved.

I never would have thought that Rose, my sweet, easygoing girl, would become so despondent that she wouldn't want to get out of bed, and that she would lay there contemplating suicide.

I never would have envisioned myself trying to stop my teen daughter Noel from running in front of a car or pulling her back from the second-floor window as she desperately tried to jump. I never would have seen myself clutching an empty pill bottle in horror ... not once, but twice.

I never would have envisioned frantic drives to the ER, not knowing what was to come, gripped with the fear that my daughter could die.

As a parent, I've been devastated to witness their emotional struggles, and I've lived in fear for their lives. It's been a rough journey ... and that is, by far, an understatement.

My children are my world, and my deepest wishes for them involve health, happiness, and the futures they've always dreamed of as a psychologist, a musician, and an environmentalist.

I want them to embrace this world and make a difference in it, each in their own way.

Suicide is the killer of dreams.

Today, I'm just happy they're alive.

I'm heartbroken for the families who have lost their children, and I grieve for them. I know we're the lucky ones. We've survived this, and my wonderful girls, Rose, Noel, and Jane, are still my greatest gifts. I'm blessed to be their mother, and I adore them to no end.

Today, having come out the other side of this, truly, I feel forged of steel—usually. I'll admit I still weep as I process the aftermath of these traumas, but overall, I do feel stronger. We've overcome the worst of this storm, and we're all the better for it. It feels like a miracle to have my girls here, alive and well.

This doesn't mean life is perfect or that we don't have work to do yet or that we never have bad days, but in my heart, I feel that we'll be okay. We've found peace and reclaimed happiness. We have hope.

My goal in writing this book is to share our journey so you know you're not alone. Within these pages, I'll share the lessons I've learned as a parent dealing with this and encourage you to find ways to better cope with your own family's situation.

I'm here to help you weather this storm and make it through in a positive, proactive, and hopeful way.

My heart goes out to you as you face your difficult days. You can do it. You're stronger than you know.

# A NOTE FROM THE AUTHOR

Please note that this is not a suicide-prevention handbook, but rather a sharing of what I've learned as a parent throughout my family's ordeal. This book originally started off as a memoir, but then it grew to include ways to empower your parenting as you navigate this time of your life.

Although I do have a BA in psychology, that doesn't make me an expert in any way, and our successes in overcoming these terrible times may or may not be the path you should take. Everyone travels their own journey, and I can't understate the importance of professional intervention as you deal with your stressors.

My three daughters have been incredibly gracious in allowing me to share their stories with you because they understand that part of my own healing is in the telling, and they believe we can help others. However, they've asked me not to use their real names.

Part I of this book takes you through our journey. In In Part II, my daughters share their experiences of feeling suicidal and what helped (and didn't help) them pull through it. Part III offers my advice for parenting a child dealing with depression or suicidality based on what I learned throughout my family's experience. Part IV lists resources you can tap into to help you get through.

As thoughts of suicide haunted my daughters, we coped with the chaos and stress as best we could. We stayed positive and proactive in attacking each problem.

We found our way back from the pits of hell. I believe you and your family can too.

IV

# Part One

MY FAMILY'S JOURNEY

# PART ONE: MY FAMILY'S JOURNEY

I don't know why I decided to sign up for the suicide-prevention class. I guess I thought that the information would be useful, "just in case." I wasn't concerned that any one of my three daughters was actually suicidal or anything. I didn't have any pressing concerns along those lines. I wasn't worried about my daughters at the moment.

Or was I?

I walked out of the class with two distinctly helpful things. The first was the knowledge that one must get help from a professional when someone acts suicidal. The second was a sheet of paper with a list of hotlines and emergency phone numbers for crisis centers in the area.

I had no idea that exactly a week later, I would be dialing one of those numbers.

# NOEL

After I separated from my husband, my three daughters and I moved to a new house in town. I knew the split was hard on them, but for the most part, they expressed their agreement about the decision.

"Things are calmer now. It's a relief," they said. "You're both much happier." Rose was eleven, Noel fourteen, and Jane sixteen.

They were feeling better about things, but unaddressed memories and emotions about what we'd been through still lingered. A lot of it seemed surreal, like it had happened to someone else.

In truth, the volatility of past events in our household and the sudden change in our family had rendered us shell-shocked.

Moving to a new home added more stress, but I hoped the new environment would offer the peace we were seeking. We all needed time to heal.

One night, a few months after the divorce was finalized, all three girls were home. Noel had a new friend over, staying the night.

"Okay, girls, I'll be back in a couple hours," I told them. I was going to a friend's baby shower.

"See you soon!" Noel called out. She and her friend were on their phones in her room.

"Bye, Mom," Rose said from another room.

"See you later," Jane said.

When I arrived at my friend's party, I made the rare decision to leave my phone in my car so I could just enjoy the party and be in the moment.

When I got back into the car, I picked up my phone and saw a missed call and a voicemail from an unknown number. I hit the play button.

"Hello, Ms. Day, this is Officer Gonzalez. I was just at your house, and I'm wondering if you could call me back as soon as possible. Thank you."

My heart seized in alarm. *What's going on?* My hands trembled as I called him back.

"Hi, Officer Gonzalez, this is Dawn Day calling you back. Is something wrong?"

"Hello, Miss Day, I just wanted you to know that your daughter Rose called 911, and I visited your house to follow up. She was concerned because there were people at your house smoking marijuana."

"What? You've got to be kidding me. That has never happened in our house. What is going on?"

"Your daughter said her sister was acting in a way that really scared her, and she couldn't get ahold of you, so she called 911."

"Okay, thanks for letting me know. I'm on my way there." I started the car and raced back home.

Jane and Rose met me at the door.

"Noel and her friend were smoking," Jane said.

"Rose, why did you call the police?" I asked. "Why didn't you wait until you could get ahold of me?"

"I was scared," she said. "The girls were acting really crazy, and it scared me. They were screaming and out of control. And Jane was making fun of them."

I glared at Jane. "I would think as the oldest in this family, you could help in this situation instead of adding to it? We'll talk more about this later."

Jane remained silent.

I walked down the hall and opened the door to Noel's room. She and her friend were sitting side by side on her bed. They looked out of it.

"Okay, where is it?" I demanded. "Give it to me, right now."

Noel's friend dug into her backpack and handed over a huge Ziploc filled with an amount of weed that shocked me.

"This is going straight down the toilet," I said and went across the hall to flush it. I couldn't believe its potency! I gagged at the overpowering smell.

"Okay, young lady, you're going home," I said to Noel's friend. "There will be no sleepover tonight."

I drove her back to her house, and when I returned, chaos had taken hold.

"You called the cops on me, Rose," Noel snarled. "I can't believe you."

"I was scared," Rose said.

"Don't you dare get on her for that," I said. "She didn't know what else to do."

A while later, Noel accosted me in the kitchen. "Do you know how I feel, Mom, every day of my life? Do you know how sad I am? How depressed? Do you know I want to die every day of my life?"

"No, Noel, I didn't. I'm sorry," I said, taken aback at her fury and shocked at her words.

"I swear I'm going to kill myself, Mom. I swear it. And you know why? Because of you. You don't help me. It's all your fault."

"Noel," I begged, "please don't say that. You know it isn't true."

"I'm in pain all the time. I just want to die!" she screamed, then ran to her room.

I chased her down the hall, terrified at what she might do.

"I need to get out of here," she said, panic rising in her voice. "Let me out!" She dove at the window and started to push on the screen, which bent dangerously outward as she pressed against it. Terrified, I envisioned her falling to the concrete driveway beneath her second-floor window.

"No!" I shouted. "What are you doing? No!" I grabbed her from behind, wrestling her away from the window. I pinned her arms and held them to her sides, pulling her back into the room. She thrashed against me.

"Let me go! I want to die!" she repeated over and over. "I want to die!" I looked up at her sisters standing frozen in the doorway.

I continued my stronghold, and eventually the thrashing stopped. I held her tightly and sobbed. "Noel, please don't jump. We love you. Please don't do it."

Noel allowed the embrace. Her body relaxed, and she started to calm down. Finally, I was able to release my hold on her.

I wanted her to sleep with me that night so I could watch over her, but she refused. With some coaxing, I was able to get her into her bed. Within a few moments, she was sound asleep.

"Mom, is she okay?" Jane asked. Rose stood rigidly beside her, not saying anything.

"Yes, she's all right. I think she had a panic attack." I encircled them in a group hug. We pressed our heads together and stood in silence for a while.

"Okay, let's get some sleep. Go to bed, and I'll watch her. I love you girls, okay? Don't forget it. We'll get through this."

# DESPERATE

After Noel fell asleep, I rushed downstairs to find the sheet of paper from the suicide-prevention class. I scanned the list for a place to call and decided on a crisis center in a nearby town. I went back upstairs to check on Noel, then placed the call from the hallway so I wouldn't wake her—although I was pretty sure she was out for the night.

"Hello, my daughter had a panic attack tonight and tried to jump out a window. I'm not sure what to do from here. Should I bring her in?"

"Is she under the influence of drugs or alcohol right now?" the intake counselor asked.

"Yes, definitely. She's not making sense, and she's not herself. She smoked something very strong." (I later found out that the potency of a lot of the marijuana sold in our area during that time had created an increase in ER visits due to the panic attacks it caused.)

"Okay, so in her current state of mind, there's likely nothing we can do for her here tonight. We wouldn't get through to her with any sort of counseling, and she wouldn't even remember it. Unless you feel she's in immediate danger?"

I looked over at her now-still form in the bed. "No, I think she'll be okay for tonight."

"Why don't you bring her first thing in the morning then."

"All right, I will. Thank you for your help."

I crossed the room to Noel's window; the frame of the screen was now bent outward. I shook my head. I sank to the floor by her bed, ready to keep watch throughout the night. She looked so peaceful right now, but the painful truth had revealed itself. Noel was in turmoil. She was suicidal, and something had to be done.

The next day, I took her to the crisis center. Although the visit stabilized her, I knew she also needed long-term help. I reached out to a local psychiatrist. The secretary had bad news.

"Our soonest available appointment is in ninety days," she said.

"What? We can't wait ninety days," I said. "She could be dead by then. This is dire. Please—can't you do anything?"

"I'm sorry, but there's really nothing we can do," she said, "except maybe put you on a waiting list for a cancellation. In the meantime, why don't you see if you can get into your primary care doctor. Maybe they can prescribe some medication."

After calling multiple other clinics and receiving the same answer, desperation overtook me. Apparently, a child feeling suicidal wasn't an urgent-enough situation to get us in. The system was too overloaded. I had no choice but to make an appointment with our primary care physician instead.

The next day, Noel and I sat together in the exam room.

"How are your periods?" the doctor asked her. "Are they normal?"

"Yeah," she said. "What does that have to do with anything?"

"There're times where it can really affect moods."

"Sir," I interjected, "this isn't just about mood swings or being a little irritable. She's had a really terrible temper, and she's also very depressed. I was hoping you could help us out with some medication, maybe, until we can get in to see a psychiatrist to figure out more."

"You know, those medications can make things worse," he said. "She'll probably get even more suicidal if she goes on anything. I wouldn't recommend it."

Anxiety rose in my chest.

Then he turned back to Noel. "If you really wanted to die, you'd be dead by now, wouldn't you?" he said harshly. "How do I know you're not faking this for attention?"

I couldn't believe it. How dare he say such a thing! Who was he to make such an assessment in five minutes? How did he know what she was feeling? I was aghast at his cold attitude.

Noel's eyes narrowed, and she stared at him with pure hatred. *Oh no.* I braced myself, certain she was about to unleash one of her rages on him. Instead, she abruptly hung her head and hid behind her curtain of long hair. She didn't say another word for the rest of the visit. She was done with him.

As we walked out the door, he looked at me and rolled his eyes in my daughter's direction, as if to say, Good luck with that.

Anger flared in me at his insensitivity. We came for help and got incompetent judgment. This had been a giant dead end in the attempt to get my suicidal daughter some help.

In the car, Noel finally spoke. "Mom, that guy was such a jerk."

"I agree. I'm sorry. I don't think he knew what to do."

She scoffed sarcastically in agreement.

*Now what?* I thought.

Mercifully, the psychiatrist's office had a cancellation shortly thereafter, and we were able to get in far sooner than the anticipated ninety days. I got a recommendation for a therapist, and Noel received some medications to help her mood swings and depression. I was relieved knowing that she was able to get some help, and I felt a little spark of hope rising within.

However, it was too little too late. These weren't magic pills that would erase all the issues. Things were about to get far, far worse for her and for our family.

# BLINDSIDED

Jane and Rose had been staying with their father that week as part of our usual custody arrangement, although for months, Noel had begun to refuse to go stay with him and had been staying with me full-time. The house felt more quiet than normal with the other two girls gone. No laughing, no sounds of the piano, cello, or harp, no speakers blaring Indie music. Strangely still. I was lying back on the bed in my bedroom, with Noel just down the hall in hers. I felt unsettled and out of sorts.

My phone dinged, and I picked it up. It was Noel texting me.

Mom come now.

*Why would she be texting me when she is right across the hall?* I felt a pit of alarm in my gut.

She was in her bed, and I immediately could tell that she was not herself. She said, "Mom, promise not to get mad . . . I did something." She pointed to her bedside, to an empty bottle of antidepressants.

I picked it up and tried to stay calm, despite my quickly rising panic. I knew it was a brand-new refill and that only one or two pills would have been taken at the most. Now, the bottle was empty . . . so she had taken twenty-eight or so, all at once.

"Get up!" I screamed.

Noel stumbled to the toilet across the hall and began to vomit.

"We need to go to the ER, now!" I shrieked.

I grabbed a pail, and we rushed out the door. Noel fell onto the seat of the car as I fumbled to put the key in the ignition. I drove to the ER in a state of shock, going as fast as I dared. Noel moaned and vomited into the pail the whole way.

"Why did you do this, Noel? Oh my god, why?"

"I don't know," she said. Her body heaved as she continued to wretch.

Surprisingly, when we got there, they did not pump her stomach because they said the vomiting had done its job as much as it could. Her heart raced at 160 beats per minute, and the doctors said that they needed to watch her.

I went around the corner from her room at the ER. I called my ex to explain to him what had just happened. After a couple of questions, he began to get agitated and started yelling at me.

"I can't do this right now," I told him and hung up on him. I knew this was his way of showing his stress, but I had reached my limit and just couldn't deal with it right now.

My legs buckled. My head fell to my hands. The enormity of this dire situation began to sink in.

"Are you all right?" asked a nurse behind the counter.

*My daughter tried to kill herself. I'm worried sick. My ex isn't being helpful, and I have to deal with this by myself.*

"Yes, I'm just fine, thank you." A complete lie.

In a little while, I got a text. My ex.

I really hope she'll be ok.

*Aha, finally, his real emotion was coming through.*

I held the phone for a few moments. I was angry with him for lashing out at me instead of showing support. It was stressful enough without adding his anger to the mix.

I stared at his text again:

I really hope she'll be ok.

I wanted to berate him for his behavior. I really wanted to let him have it. But now wasn't the time. She was our daughter, and she was in peril.

I texted back:

Me too.

# ALTERNATE REALITY

Noel's heart raced all night long.

In the morning, the ER doctor gave me a report. "Her heart rate is still around 160 beats per minute, so we're going to admit her to the hospital. Normally we would be releasing her to the mental health facility, but we need to be sure she's medically stable first."

The staff wheeled her to the elevator and took her upstairs to her room.

As Noel's body processed the excess medicine, intense hallucinations overtook her mind. She babbled incoherently.

Her nurse simply nodded at her nonsensical ramblings. "You see a frog jumping? Well, that's interesting," she said. She had a round, motherly figure and a thick foreign accent I couldn't place. I appreciated her warmth and ready acceptance of the situation.

Noel got out of the hospital bed and approached the wall, staring at it.

"Look, there's a funny little man here." She laughed, eyes crinkling.

"Where do you see that?" I asked.

"Right here," she said, pointing at the thermometer.

The nurse and I exchanged a rueful smile, but the underlying situation didn't warrant humor.

She pointed across the room. "SpongeBob is right over there!"

As the day went by, her hallucinations morphed into more menacing beings.

"There are worms all over the floor! They're crawling everywhere!"

A while later, "There's a man trying to get me! Help me, Mama!" Terrified, she jumped into my lap. Violent shaking wracked her body.

"It's okay, Noel. It's going to be okay," I said, holding her and gently rubbing her back.

She looked up at me. Her face softened, and she patted my cheek. She said simply, "Mom," and smiled sweetly. Then she whipped her head around and pointed at the nurse across the room.

"That woman! Her face is melting!" she cried.

"No, no, Noel, it's not melting. It's the nurse. She's here to help you."

"Something's wrong with her face! It doesn't look right!"

"It's okay, honey. It's okay. I promise. It's just the nurse," I repeated. "She won't hurt you. She's nice, see? I'm here with you, and I won't let anything happen to you. Okay?"

She clung to me and started shaking again. I continued to soothe her and rub her back.

Eventually, she calmed down, although her hallucinations continued.

"Why don't you go home and take a shower, and maybe have a nap?" the nurse suggested to me. "I know you haven't had a break. I promise I'll look after her."

"All right," I agreed reluctantly. As I left, she and Noel sat across from each other, working on a coloring book. Walking out, I could hear Noel's voice as she continued to regale the nurse with her mind-altered tales.

When I returned a few hours later, the two of them were in the hallway by the nurses' station, back from a walk together around the hospital wing.

"Look, there's a dragon over there!" Noel declared. "It's right there!" Several nurses' eyes shifted to where she was pointing, but I was sure they'd pretty much seen it all at this point. An invisible dragon didn't faze them.

Later that day, Noel's father and sisters came to visit. Jane and Rose watched wide-eyed as their sister alternated between delight and fright.

"Did you hear that? Did you hear what she said?" Noel asked, pointing at the nurse as her face contorted in paranoid disbelief. No one was saying a word.

Her sisters looked at me uncertainly.

"Why is she saying that?" Rose whispered.

"It's the meds she took, honey," I explained. "They're causing hallucinations."

"Will she be all right, Mom?" Jane asked.

"Yes, she'll be okay," I said reassuringly, even though deep down, I had no idea.

What good would it do for me to be frank with them right now?

I regretted my decision to have them come and see her in this state of mind—it only added to their fear. And certainly, the visit did nothing for Noel. She was too tripped out to even remember it. I never should've let them come.

That night, another nurse was assigned to watch over Noel. I appreciated her sweet and supportive nature. She filled me in on what was going on.

"Her heart rate is still much too high. Otherwise, we would have discharged her to the residential treatment facility by now."

We tried to get Noel to lie down in the bed, but she remained restless. She kept seeing things. "There are snakes in the bed! Look, there! I see them!" she said as she flinched away.

"There are sheets here and a pillow. That's all," soothed the nurse. "See?"

But Noel's eyes darted around, looking here, looking there, seeing things that didn't exist. Sleep eluded her in this state of agitation.

We dimmed the lights. I rubbed her back gently and sang softly to her.

"Hush, little baby, don't say a word. Mama's gonna buy you a mockingbird. And if that mockingbird don't sing, Mama's gonna buy you a diamond ring . . ." I didn't remember all the words, so I drifted off into humming the melody instead.

As a little girl at bedtime, she would say, "Rub my back, Mama." When I would eventually stop, she would beg me to continue. Here I was, rubbing my little girl's back, just like I used to. Except now, she was a teenager who had taken a bottle of pills.

*Because she had tried to die.*

Bereft, I stood by her bedside, continuing to rub her back.

Slowly, she started to calm down. Her eyes fluttered closed, and at last she fell asleep. I prayed for a restorative slumber—without nightmares—and for the distressing hallucinations to end.

"I know this has been hard," the nurse said. "Why don't you lie down on the cot there and get some rest while you can? I'll watch her for you. I promise to wake you if anything happens."

I eased my leaden body onto the mattress, my head sinking into the pillow. From across the dimly lit room, Noel's long, dark curls contrasted against the white sheets. The computer screen on the bedside cart illuminated the nurse's face as she prepared to keep vigil throughout the night.

I turned over and stared at the wall as the recent events replayed in my mind. The pill bottle with nothing left, the jolting shock, the violent vomiting, the chaos in the ER, the freakish hallucinations. The professionals who dipped in and out of our hellish nightmare.

*Will Noel survive this? Will she try again? How will we keep her safe?*

*Will our lives ever be the same again?*

I kept staring at the wall, thinking and processing. Finally, the emotional exhaustion overtook me, and sleep mercifully swept me away.

# HIDDEN WORLD

In the morning, I stood by Noel's bedside as she slept. The bed engulfed her thin body.

*She's still breathing.*

Her eyes fluttered open. "Hi, Mom," she said drowsily.

She recognized me! Her hallucinations had subsided.

"Hi, honey," I said, smoothing her tousled curls. "How are you feeling?"

"I'm all right," she said.

The doctor came in the room. She checked Noel's chart, then turned to me. "Okay, her heart rate's down, which is a good thing. We can medically clear her now. She's going to go to a psychiatric facility, but I'm sorry to say that she'll have to go down to Broomfield, about an hour away."

"What? Why so far?"

"Mountain Crest is full. They only have eight beds there. There's a shortage of psych beds in this area."

I couldn't believe this could be true of such an economically vibrant region.

*So, there are at least eight other kids going through this right now. Eight other families are stressed out and petrified for their sons and daughters.*

And that was just in our corner of the world, just today. One of the attendants in the ER had told me they dealt with at least one case of someone trying to take their own life almost every night. They expected it. They knew how to deal with it.

This was very new territory for us.

The nurse said, "You can't drive her there yourself. She'll have to be escorted to the facility by a police officer."

"The police!" I protested. "Why? She hasn't done anything illegal!"

"It's a required measure to keep her safe en route."

I clamped my mouth shut against further protests.

I helped Noel change into plain blue scrubs. The nurse wheeled her out of the room, into the elevator, and down to the curb.

The assigned officer stood by the police car. He nodded to me. "I'll take care of her. Don't worry," he said.

"Thank you," I said. I marveled at the many hats officers often had to wear. Today he was on suicide watch. With Noel.

Noel got out of the wheelchair, and the officer guided her into the back seat. A metal grid separated the front and back seats, like a cage. I leaned over to say goodbye.

"I'll pick up some of your things and be there soon. I love you, honey," I said.

Her dark-gray eyes looked huge in her pale, gaunt face. "Goodbye, Mama," she said. Her voice sounded small and far away.

I stepped aside and watched the surreal scene as the police car took my little girl away.

*She's a prisoner. She's lost the right to make her own choices.* Others were in control of her life right now, at least for the next seventy-two hours—the mandatory time she needed to stay under the care of professionals.

I went home to pack Noel's things. I'd been told I couldn't pack anything sharp, and no belts were allowed, or strings in her hoodies, lest these items be used for self-harm.

My phone rang. It was my friend Kim, whose daughter had been close to Noel since first grade.

"Dawn, what's going on with Noel? Regan just told me she posted a photo of herself in the back of a police car?"

"What?" I replied, shocked. "Are you kidding me?" I filled her in briefly on recent events.

"Okay," Kim said, "you need to be aware of what's been going on with Noel online. Regan just told me you should see what's going on in this private Instagram group she's in. I'll give you Regan's login info so you can see."

"Thank you so much for telling me. I'll keep you posted," I said.

I opened the app and entered Regan's login information.

There it was: a photo of Noel in the police car, clearly clothed in a set of scrubs. Beneath it she had written, "Rough day in the hood. Having a hard day."

*I can't believe she shared this publicly. What is she thinking?* I read through some of the responses. Most were sympathetic, but some were dismissive and even cruel. None of the names seemed familiar, and I didn't see any of her friends in the profile pictures. Some of the names had swear words embedded in them. *Who are these people?*

I scrolled down the feed of the group to see what they were talking about and sharing. I stopped, shocked, on image after image.

One photo showed someone pouring bleach into a drinking glass. Someone had commented, "Drink bleach, bitch!" followed by a heart emoji. *I love you; now go kill yourself.*

Another photo showed a man pointing a gun to his head and laughing.

Photos, quotes, memes, emojis . . . all making light of killing yourself.

The theme of the group seemed to be, "Isn't suicide so funny? It's hilarious—a big joke . . . *so* not a big deal. Why don't we form a pact? It might be fun!"

These strangers were encouraging my child to go ahead and pull that trigger, drink that bleach, take those pills—go for it. And she'd done just that.

*Was this group the reason Noel had tried to end her life?*

Discovering what had been going on behind closed doors, just feet away from me, right under my nose, sickened me. I felt like I'd invited a dangerous gang of strangers off the street to come into our home without even knowing it. It shook me to my core. My stomach seized, and I couldn't catch my breath.

I knew I'd have to deal with this online situation, but Noel's emotional state was precarious right now; it wasn't the time for confrontations. Fortunately, she wasn't allowed to have a phone at the psychiatric facility, and I vowed to strictly limit her phone time when she came home.

# DESPAIR

The following day, Rose and I drove to Broomfield—a two-hour round trip—to see Noel for just an hour, the only time allotted during daily visitation. Although it was hard to be away from her, it was a relief to know that, at least for now, she was being supervised around the clock. I was anxious about the upcoming responsibility of keeping her safe at home.

Rose was excited to see her sister. "How are you doing, sis?" she asked in her usual sweet, gentle manner.

"I wish I'd died," Noel said bluntly. "I don't want to be here anymore."

Rose's eyes widened in shock. Her face crumpled.

"You can't mean that, Noel," I said.

"Yes, I do. I want to be dead. I wish I'd died," she repeated.

Rose was too upset to speak; she stayed silent for the remainder of the visit.

On the ride home, I tried to console her. "It's hard to see your sister that way. I know. It's just going to take time."

"I don't want her to die, Mama," she said, her voice breaking.

"I know," I said and shook my head sadly. "I don't either. We've just got to have faith that she can get better. I know it seems bad right now. But she's getting help. That's something." I squeezed her hand.

She turned and looked out into the night as tears streamed down her face. My poor baby girl. Just eleven years old and hurting so much for her sister, so afraid. And Jane—so heartbroken, desperately worried for Noel, and lately, deeply depressed herself. My heart ached for the pain our family was going through. This didn't just affect Noel; it affected us all.

The next day, I went to visit Noel again. She was in the common room of the facility, hunched on a chair, arms wrapped around her knees, hair hanging like a protective cloak around her fragile form. She could barely get through a sentence without breaking down and weeping.

My heart wrenched to see her so distraught. My sweet girl was struggling. Depression threatened to pull her down into nothingness.

I didn't know how we were going to keep her alive.

# EVIL

Noel was set to be released in a couple of days, after a week at the facility. I was faced with the daunting prospect of keeping her from harming herself. Our home, once a safe haven, now harbored countless potential dangers.

Now it was our turn to be on suicide watch, meaning that I had to figure out everything possible to keep her safe.

I knew some of the basics at least, like locking away knives and chemicals—I'd had a carpenter build a locked cabinet in the garage for those items while Noel was away. We didn't have guns in the house, so that was one less thing to worry about.

The people at the facility advised me to leave Noel's bedroom door open at all times once she was home. If she refused to comply, they said to take the door off its hinges. That way I could supervise her actions constantly.

But even with all this advice, I still wanted to be sure I wasn't missing anything. My friend Shelley came over to help me make the house safe. We didn't know where to begin, so we did an online search. Surely we could find a resource to help parents with this task.

We sat side by side at my laptop, and I typed in *how to suicide proof your house*. The first search result was a website called How to Kill Yourself.

Our eyes locked, and our jaws dropped in disbelief. Mortified, I clicked the link. The website offered a top-ten list of ways to end your life, complete with detailed instructions: you could drink X amount of bleach or Y amount of window cleaner. Ingest Z amount of this kind of glue.

On and on it went, detailing the best ways to kill yourself. Cheerful black-and-white sketches with pops of color depicted each lighthearted-looking scenario. One scene depicted a fun little cocktail party, each of the attendees smiling widely and holding a martini glass filled with blue liquid ... window cleaner. Beneath the sketch was a helpful annotation of the exact number of ounces you'd need to consume to ensure your death.

"Oh my god." It's all we could say for minutes on end. "Oh my god. Oh my god. Oh my god!"

We clutched each other's hand and wept.

What kind of sick person creates a website that not only encourages someone to die but specifically instructs them on how to do it? How many deaths had this caused?

It's one thing to have a child who wants to die, but it's another entirely to know there are people out there cheering them on and telling them to go for it. It sickened me. And as we went on to discover, this website was one of many. To know that someone—much less multiple people—would prey upon a child's emotional despondency to encourage them to go through with it ... it's beyond cruel. It's evil.

After some more research, Shelley and I finally figured out our plan of attack. We decided to start in Noel's room.

I knew it was best to do this now rather than wait until Noel was home. She was a walking tinderbox these days; it took nothing to ignite her angry tirades. Her intense and erratic emotions created a minefield for me as a parent. If we rifled through her things while she was there, she would lose it.

Shelley and I started in the closet, going through backpacks and other miscellaneous items to ensure they didn't contain anything dangerous or sharp. On the top shelf, I spotted a half-empty gallon of vodka. A gallon!

"Oh, no," I said, holding up the bottle. "You know, she's been throwing up a lot lately, and I thought it was a reaction to these new meds. Great."

I rarely drank, so I hadn't noticed it was missing from the dining-room hutch. I never would've dreamed that Noel would help herself to it. Again, so naïve. Right under my nose.

I sighed heavily. She was only fourteen. What were we in for in the future if she was already doing this stuff now? What a mess. Things were happening fast.

The drinking was probably her way of trying to make herself feel better, to numb her emotional pain. For the moment, it was less important than her suicide attempt.

We continued, searching beneath the bed and everywhere else we could think of. I opened the top drawer of her dresser and gasped.

"What? What is it?" Shelley asked in alarm.

"Oh, no," I said again in complete dismay.

The front of the drawer was full of a variety of sharp things. There were safety pins, razor blades, and several jagged pieces of broken glass. Broken glass!

I knew why they were there.

"She's been 'cutting,'" I said. "I knew she was doing this. I've seen marks all over her arm. She won't stop."

Shelley put her hand to her mouth. "Oh, Dawn, I'm so sorry," she said. "I can't believe this. I've heard of kids doing this, but I don't get it."

I sank to the floor and propped my back up against the dresser.

Shelley sat cross-legged in front of me.

"The therapists have told me it's a way some kids release pain. They almost make it sound like it's an okay thing to do. I guess when you think of what she just did—trying to kill herself—cutting doesn't seem as bad. But I don't get this at all! This whole thing! When we were growing up, did kids do this? It wouldn't have even occurred to us! They're hurting themselves on purpose. I don't get it."

"I don't either," she said. "The internet! That's where they're getting all these ideas."

"Yes," I said. "It's like they create this culture of acceptance. They glorify this whole thing about hurting yourself, and they make it cool. It's all unsupervised—a bunch of bullying and completely inappropriate behavior. No parents anywhere, no guidance. It takes on a direction of its own. Look at the website we just found! Prime example."

"Does Noel know that you know she's doing this?"

"Yes, she does. I've confronted her about it. We've talked to the therapist. She's totally embarrassed that I know she's doing it, and she wears long sleeves all the time. Obviously, she can't stop herself for whatever reason. I'm afraid she'll have scars for life."

"I'm so, so sorry," Shelley said.

"This whole thing makes me so sad," I said, my voice breaking. "I never saw any of it coming. She tried to die! And now she's in a place with total strangers that I have to trust. She's not even herself anymore. She gets angry, and it scares me. Then she cries and can't handle anything at all. It's heartbreaking to see her like this. I have no idea how it got this bad. It's just a nightmare."

My shoulders sagged and tears rolled down my cheeks as my dear friend did the only thing she could: hear me out, offer consolation, and urge me to continue our mission to help keep my daughter safe from her own self.

After I'd regained my composure, Shelley said, "All right, let's get back to work."

It took us the entire day to go through every cupboard and drawer in the house. Each individual item was considered. Was this sharp enough to do damage? Could this be used to strangulate? Would this be fatal if ingested? Could this normally harmless item be used to harm oneself? Or this one? Or this, or this, or this? Everything in the house was evaluated in turn. It was a painstaking process.

We found a host of chemicals in the kitchen, bathrooms, and garage. We placed everything I needed for daily use in the cabinet the carpenter had built. A separate locked chest housed the lesser-used chemicals and household sharps. We secured both with combination-style padlocks.

A special lockbox in the kitchen held cooking knives and scissors. Another locked box held Noel's meds. I had a hard time finding something specifically for this purpose (nothing came up in a search for *locked meds box*), and after some head-scratching and research, I ended up settling for a hard-plastic ammo box with a three-digit slider code on the front. A piece of paper with all the codes was hidden away where I thought that she would never find it.

At the end of the day, I sent Shelley off with a box of chemicals I didn't have room for in the cabinet or chest, including several bottles of bleach. After seeing the pro-suicide meme with the bleach being poured into the drinking glass, I never wanted to see any in my house again.

"Thank you, friend," I said, hugging her fiercely. "You're an angel. You earned your wings today."

After Shelley left, I thought more about how online access has so adversely affected children. I should've monitored what my girls were doing online. Those outside influences do nothing to help a teen who is already perched on the precipice of suicide. In an already-fragile state of mind, it only takes the tiniest nudge to go over that edge.

Our family was now a part of the statistics you hear about, but we weren't just a number. To us, the nightmare was very real.

We were to live it for a long time to come.

# IN GOD'S HANDS

Two months later, I got a call from a counselor assigned by our health insurance company.

"Your daughter Noel had a suicide attempt about two months ago, is that right?"

"Yes. Eight weeks ago today."

"How's it going?"

"I think she's doing so much better!" I said. "I'm so encouraged. She's home right now since we're doing half-day homeschooling. We thought it would help her get through since she was struggling to make it through the school day. She spent a week at the psychiatric facility, and that seemed to stabilize her. She has a great counselor now who she seems to like."

"That's great to hear," the counselor said. "Is she in any other type of programs?"

"Yes," I said. "She's in an intensive outpatient program three days a week, three hours each session. She likes the other kids there, and it helps her to know she's not the only one going through this. They ride horses and talk about emotion management. And I really love the man who runs it. He's so wise and calming, and there's a parent program he runs too. I did that, and it helped me a lot."

"Has she told you if she's feeling any better lately?" the counselor asked.

"Just last night she came up to me and said, 'I feel so good right now.' She said it was the best she's felt in a long time," I replied.

"That's great."

We continued talking, and the counselor gave me one last piece of advice. "A lot of times, they seem like they're getting better, but then there's a setback. Don't be surprised if anything like that happens."

I truly doubted what she was saying. Noel was doing so well—surely we were over the worst of it.

I thanked her as we ended the call. I was so grateful to have professionals surrounding me with their knowledge and support. I took a deep breath. Things seemed to be turning around.

An hour later, I received a text from one of my daughter's friends:

You need to go check on Noel. She is saying goodbye to everyone.

*No!*

I raced downstairs to find her sleeping on the couch, curled up in a ball underneath a comforter. I shook her firmly. "Wake up!"

She barely stirred.

My hearted started hammering, and my mouth went dry. "Wake up!" I shouted, shaking her harder.

She opened her eyes.

"What's going on?" I demanded.

Her eyelids drooped, and she didn't respond.

Then I saw it: another empty pill bottle. How could this have happened? Just two minutes ago, I had seen the locked meds box in the kitchen.

"What did you do?" I cried. "How did you get to this?"

"It was only a three-digit code," she said, her speech slurred. "I figured it out. I researched how many pills it would take, and that's how many I took."

"Rose, come here now!" I shouted.

Rose rushed into the room, bewildered as Noel stumbled to her feet.

"Go to Stephanie's right now and stay there," I said to Rose. "Tell her I'm going to the hospital with Noel."

Terrified, Rose nodded and didn't say a word.

It was a repeat of the first chaotic scenario. As we pulled out of the driveway, I saw Rose going into our neighbor's house next door. I drove frantically to the ER.

After the first suicide attempt, I tried to be calm. I offered gentle support and compassion. This time, anger raged through me.

"What are you doing? I don't understand! *Why?*"

We made it to the ER, and I spent another endless night there, worried sick for her. I sat by her bed, watching the attendants take her vitals, my bleary eyes scanning the monitors. I slept restlessly in my chair, waking often to see if anything had changed, worried that something could happen.

In the middle of the night, one of the ER doctors approached me. "I need to tell you something," he said.

A deep sense of dread seized me. "What is it?"

"Noel's heart has an arrhythmia." He paused.

"So, what does that mean?"

"It's a signal that means her heart could stop beating."

I stared at him, unwilling to accept his words.

"We'll keep watching her throughout the night," he said, putting his hand on my shoulder briefly and then walking away.

*Her heart could stop beating.*

I collapsed into the chair. The reality sunk in: Noel could die. Suddenly, the anger I'd been feeling exploded, burning through my body. So, this was going to be it then? I was going to lose my child like this? I was so angry with her. Why did she do this? Why did she want to leave us?

I'd done everything possible to try to help her, to keep her safe, get professional help, take away stress, monitor her. And she'd still tried to do it, right under my nose. What more could I have done? Things were out of my control right now; there was nothing I could do. I knew that no matter what happened, I would have no choice but to accept the outcome.

Agony seared through my soul. It was more than I could handle on my own. In my state of utter helplessness, I gave it up to God.

"Please, God, help her get through this," I prayed. "Please let her live. We can't lose her. We can't."

I sobbed by her bedside. I gazed down at my precious girl, stroked her hair, held her hands in mine. I thought of all the things I loved about her: her spunky nature, her sense of humor, her little ringlets and huge blue eyes when she was a baby, bouncing up and down in the bouncy seat. Her sweet little voice. Her soft little hands.

Throughout the night, I heard the beep, beep, beep of the monitors, terrified for her life, dreading the moment I would hear the flatline.

Minutes crept by. Hours came. The sun rose. Another day passed. Incredibly, miraculously, she stabilized. I stared incredulously at the monitors. As life crept back into my daughter's heart, hope leapt back into mine. Noel had survived, again.

*Another chance at life.*

# JANE

Before I had children, I never doubted I'd be a good parent one day. I was a teacher, and that had shaped me into a master guider and disciplinarian. I knew my way around kids, and I understood them.

When my kids were little, I would look at other families whose kids were on drugs or emotionally unstable, and I fully admit that I thought there was no way my kids would ever be like *that*. Surely those parents must have done something wrong. We would have a great family, and those kinds of issues would never befall us.

I always thought, *I know my children will never be one of the "messed-up" ones.*

I was *so* wrong.

In truth, as I've learned, mental illness can strike any family, and it's often brought on by outside stressors or a genetic predisposition. It's something we should address, not sweep under the rug. It isn't something that should bring us shame. Yet it does.

My oldest daughter, Jane, had suffered from extreme mood swings for years. Depression dove in and out of her life, but her passion for music always kept her afloat . . . until something happened to create a raging crest that threatened to pull her under for good.

About two years after Noel's second suicide attempt, Jane had just gone off to college and was living an hour from home, studying music on a scholarship.

One day, she came home for a visit.

"It's so great to have you here," I said, hugging her. "We miss you so much."

"I miss you too."

"How's school going? Do you love it or what?" I asked, certain she would say yes.

"Mom, I need to tell you something," she said instead. "Come sit with me." I joined her at the kitchen table.

"What's going on?" I asked.

"This is hard to tell you, Mom." Trepidation tightened my chest.

"Okay, honey, just tell me." I held my breath while she gathered her courage.

"I was raped," she blurted.

"Oh my god!" I cried. "Who? Where?"

"It was a boy that I met at school. He came to my room."

"You invited him there?" I asked.

"Yes, I did."

"So was this consensual then? What are you saying?"

"It was . . . at first. But then . . ." Her voice trailed off, and she shook her head.

I leaned forward intently. "Tell me what happened. I need to understand."

"All I can tell you is that I did invite him there, and I did want him there," she said, "but there came a point where it became scary for me. He was there all night, and he didn't leave."

"Why didn't you ask him to leave? It was your place, and you had a right to do that."

"I think I was so traumatized by everything that I was numb and didn't know how to respond. And it only hit me later on how bad it all was."

Anger knocked me sideways. My daughter had attended college all of a month before something like this had happened. Was date rape so prevalent at college that it was inevitable?

"I don't understand why young boys are no different today than they ever were. You would think things would be better now. That young men wouldn't be treating women like sex objects. That there would be some change in our society by now. It sickens me." My whole body shook.

"It has everything to do with online pornography," she told me. "You wouldn't believe what's out there. What these boys are seeing. It's setting up expectations of what they should be expecting from women sexually. Sometimes there's violence." I couldn't bring myself to ask if that was part of her experience. I was deathly afraid to find out.

"It's disgusting. You've got to file charges," I urged.

"No!" she snapped. "No, I won't!"

"Have you seen a counselor? Isn't this what they're saying to do?"

"Yes, I have seen one at school, and she said I should, but I don't have to. I'm not doing it. I don't want to see him ever again."

"Jane, I can't believe that you wouldn't do this. You're so big on women's rights, and why wouldn't you want to do this to protect someone else from being hurt too? I don't get it."

"Mom, I'm not doing it. I can't. And it's my choice."

"I'm flabbergasted, honestly. You should! He'll do it again!"

"No," she said resolutely. "I'm not doing it."

"Okay, I'll let it go for now. I'm so sorry for what you're going through." I hugged her fiercely and cried as the situation began to sink in. "Are you going to be okay?"

I was so heartbroken for what my daughter had been through. This poor girl went to take on the world, only to fall victim to one of its many evils.

"I think it will just take time to get over it," she said. "But I'm okay. I think I'll be fine."

# BLAME

Later, I called a friend and confided what had happened to Jane.

"Did she invite him over?" she asked.

"Yes, she did."

"Well, what's the problem then?" she asked.

"She didn't know it would get so out of control."

"Well, she shouldn't have invited him over then, I guess," she said.

"You think this is her fault? Wow." I paused, shocked by her lack of compassion. "You know what, I'll talk to you later. I gotta go." I hung up.

I put my head in my hands. *Why?* Why did people do this to victims? Why were people so heartless? Why were rapists repeatedly given the benefit of the doubt and women disbelieved?

Throughout my life, I'd heard comments from many others who placed blame on women for their rapes: "Well, what did she expect? She dresses so provocatively," and, "You can't expect a man to stop." Or, "She should have known better. She really needs to wise up."

Just like what my friend was saying.

*Wrong, so wrong.* And now it was directed at my own daughter. My friend's words and harsh judgment crushed me.

That night, I lay in my bed as grief washed over me. I clutched my pillow and sobbed, thinking of all my girl had gone through already at such a young age. Anger poured out of me for the unfairness of it. All her boundaries had been plowed down, both physically and emotionally.

My mind went back to a memory of her as a toddler in the baby swing, blond ringlets backlit by the sun on a carefree summer day, laughing, begging me to keep going.

"Again, Mama, again!" she cried.

"All right, here we go! Wheeee!" I would push her again, and she would shriek in delight every time. Such innocent days.

Today, she was a young woman shattered. I grieved the loss of her innocence. I grieved the fact that her traumatic experience was only worsened by the harsh judgment of others with no sympathy for what she went through. Such a cruel, cruel world. My heart ached for my daughter's pain. Once again, I felt powerless to help.

# CRUMBLING

Little by little, over the next year, Jane's emotional stability began to crumble.

When she came home for Christmas, she broke down and cried repeatedly and uncontrollably. I could see she was unraveling, but with her already in therapy and not living close to home, it was hard for me to do much more. She was an adult now, and I had less control over the situation than I did with Noel.

But having been through what we went through with Noel, I was worried for Jane too. I knew we were skirting dangerous ground.

"Are you having suicidal thoughts?" I asked her.

"No. I'm okay," she said.

She was not okay.

After Christmas, my boyfriend, John, and I were scheduled to drive his parents from Maine to their winter home in Florida while the girls visited their father. Part of me felt like I should stay home, but Jane had returned to her apartment, and John and I had already purchased our flights.

After a few days' travel, we had just one more day to go before arriving in Florida. I was lying in bed in a hotel room in Virginia when my cell phone rang.

It was Jane, back in Colorado. "Mom, I'm having a really hard time right now. I'm not doing well at all."

I shot upright in the bed. Dread swept across me like a sickness.

"What's going on?"

"I can't do this anymore, Mom. I'm not doing well. I can't handle it! I want to die. I don't know what to do."

"Don't do anything! Promise me!" I said. "You need to call the crisis center Noel went to. Promise me you'll hang up and do it right now. Then I want you to call me right back."

Jane called me back. "Okay, they have a bed opening up in the morning."

"Oh, what a relief. That's good," I said. "I'm going to get a plane back home as soon as I can, okay? Hang in there. Promise me you won't do anything."

"I promise, Mom," she said.

I hung up and put my head in my hands. We were facing a suicide crisis, again.

The next day, my friend Karen picked me up from the airport and drove me straight to the crisis center so we could get there in time for the one hour of visitation allowed each day. I couldn't wait to see Jane.

Karen and I had been dear friends since our children were in kindergarten. She knew our family well.

"I'm so sorry to hear about what's going on with Jane," she said in the car. "You've all been through so much already."

"I know. It's been so hard," I said. "I'm just so worried about her. She's falling apart."

"When I think of Jane," she said, "I think of this sweet little blond, curly-haired girl out on the playground, running around out there with this big smile. This kind-hearted girl, so happy. It's hard for me to think of her any other way."

"She's still that girl—we just can't find her right now. She's in a lot of pain," I said. "It's just heartbreaking." I shook my head and could no longer speak.

I looked out the window at the Rocky Mountains, steadfast and imposing on the western horizon. Their familiar presence offered me solace.

*These mountains have seen more than I have. This is just a moment in time. Fleeting. Just like all the other moments of all the other humans on Earth, it will come, and it will go.*

*But will Jane still be alive when it does?*

# DIGGING DEEP

Jane spent five days at the crisis center. The doctors there dug deep, but she was honest with them and told them everything she'd been feeling. I called her every day during her stay.

"I'm really trying to get better, Mom," she said. "I promise."

The first step was agreeing to go on medication. This was something she'd resisted her entire life. It was a sign that she was no longer resisting what could help her.

"I think I'm really starting to figure some things out," she told me on one of our calls. "I'll tell you more about it when I get back."

When she returned home, we sat together to look through her paperwork.

"Look at this, Mom," she said.

I took a paper from her hands. On it was an illustration of a tree showing roots on the bottom and leaves on the top.

"It's called the tree of shame," she explained. "The roots are the things that are causing you to feel shame, and the leaves are the ways it's showing up in your behavior."

The roots listed things like divorce, abuse, abandonment, poverty, imprisonment, neglect, trauma, bullying, ridicule, and isolation. The leaves had the ways that shame manifests: anxiety, depression, pleasing, perfectionism, blaming, fear, violence, abuse of substances, promiscuity, eating disorders, workaholism, and suicide.

"What does this illustration mean to you personally?" I asked. "I mean, what do you see as your root causes for some of the things you're going through?"

Jane pointed to two different words. The first was *trauma*.

"The rape," she said.

I put my hand on hers. "I'm so sorry, honey," I said. "I wish I could make things better for you. I've got to rely on your therapists for helping you through that part because I really don't know how this gets treated. I'm here for you if you want to talk about it."

The second word she pointed to was *abuse*.

"Growing up," she said simply. It's the first time she'd ever used this word to describe her childhood experiences—at least with me.

I paused. "The yelling? The anger?"

"Yes," she said. "I always felt like I was doing something wrong. I got jumpy and nervous. After a while, I had really bad anxiety. I was always afraid."

Our eyes met, and memories passed silently between us. Road-rage incidents with her father at the wheel and three terrified little girls in the back seat. Public chastisement in front of strangers as he harshly reprimanded the girls for perceived infringements. His black rages precipitated by minor events. Terrible memories.

*My poor girl. It's my fault. Why did I stay in a household of rage? Why didn't I foresee the emotional devastation?*

Here was my daughter, processing these childhood memories even now, at the age of twenty. Incidents so far in her past still affected her deeply. The effects of her trauma lingered.

My shoulders drooped under the crushing weight of my regrets. I had so many. The answers didn't clearly reveal themselves to me back then, and nothing was black and white. What could I do at this point except accept how things were now? I couldn't change the past. I could only move forward to help her through as best I could.

Jane handed me another piece of paper with all the diagnoses they'd come up with at the center. I was shocked to see how many afflictions were listed. There were diagnoses here that we'd never known. This was the first time in her life anyone had put labels on it.

It hit me then, hard. My daughter was sick. She was mentally ill, and she was suffering. Why hadn't I understood this before now?

The emotional intensity that allowed her to fly high in her passion for music, for example, also threw her deep into the well of despair at times. When her emotions were positive, she thrived; when they weren't, she suffered.

She had struggled emotionally at different points in her life, then she'd get better as the stressors eased. I would breathe a sigh of relief, thinking she was better now and was going to get through.

But the down times would always return—because she wasn't getting better. She was only pushing down her feelings. She was haunted repeatedly by these emotional demons, and the unaddressed angst would rise to the surface time and again.

One of the diagnoses on the list was familiar to me; her father had been diagnosed with the very same thing. I had also been intensely emotional at her age. I'd had massive mood swings, I was quick to anger, and I was overly sensitive. The rest of my family walked on eggshells around me.

Unfortunately, some of this was inherited.

I took the list and began some heavy-duty researching to try to understand what each of these diagnoses meant. As I dug deeper, I saw that the descriptions of the behaviors really did match how she was acting.

At first, I was surprised to see post-traumatic stress disorder (PTSD) on the list. For Jane, the traumas from both her childhood and the recent rape had combined with a vengeance, now demanding to be acknowledged.

"The rape has been more traumatic than I thought," she told me. "And the trauma gets worse over time. I'm having nightmares. I relive what happened over and over."

I learned that with PTSD, reliving the memories eventually becomes worse than experiencing the trauma itself.

*No wonder she couldn't stop crying at Christmas and couldn't get herself from one day to the next. No wonder she couldn't focus in class or make it through this semester. She was in a state of traumatic stress.*

Now, I understood much more clearly what was happening.

It was helpful to put names to the faces of her afflictions and better understand her mental breakdowns. I chose to look at her diagnoses as identifiers of the issues at hand; if we could identify it, we could understand what it was, what factors might have brought it on, and what could be done to address it. That was incredibly empowering.

It was a start, although the real work was yet to come.

# GOODBYE LETTERS

Jane's time in the crisis center seemed to stabilize her, but only for a time. A few months later, she was feeling suicidal again.

She texted me:

I need to come home now. I am not doing well.

She came home and threw her duffel bag on the floor. I hugged her fiercely. "We'll get you through this."

"Life sucks right now, Mom. I'm struggling really bad. But I want to get help."

After we talked for a while, it became clear that she needed to return to the crisis center. Jane picked up her phone and called them. I overheard part of her conversation.

"Yes, I have been thinking about it," she told them. "Yes, there's things here that I could do it with." She paused. "I've been writing letters to everyone I love, to say goodbye."

The staff had heard enough to know she should come back for another stay.

While Jane was admitted, I visited my ex.

"We need to talk about Jane," I told him. "I think we need to do something more for her. I feel like she goes into this crisis center, gets shored up, feels better for a while, but then it's not enough to sustain her. I think we need to find something more intensive. If something doesn't change, we're going to lose her." I started to cry. "It's so heartbreaking to see her so sad."

We talked for two straight hours. In truth, I was proud of the way we could co-parent when we needed to come together for our children. This was certainly one of those times.

We thought about putting her into a particular outdoor-adventure therapy program. She loved nature, and we thought it might be a good solution. But it was tens of thousands of dollars, and they didn't accept insurance. So, that option was off the table.

Later, we reached out to Jane's college, which had assigned her a social worker and a caseworker. I was amazed that they had such resources available to us. They helped us research potential options. We decided to do an intensive outpatient program that included three hours of dialectical behavior therapy (DBT) three days a week for eight weeks. DBT was supposed to have a high success rate in helping suicidal teens and young adults.

When Jane returned from the second crisis center visit, she couldn't fathom picking up a phone, or emailing anyone, or doing anything to help herself. She was far too depressed, overloaded, and overwhelmed. I knew I would have to take the wheel for a while.

"Why don't you call work and ask for a leave of absence?" I suggested. She had a part-time job while attending school. Her employer was more than willing to work with her.

I sat with her, and we made phone calls, filled out paperwork, and did everything needed to get her enrolled in the program. We drove an hour to the facility to get the initial intake done, and from there, because of COVID-19, the course was online.

I called the dean at her college to see if she could take a semester or a year off yet still retain her scholarship. She was a gifted harpist, having earned this scholarship after only a year of playing the instrument.

"My daughter Jane is struggling emotionally right now," I told him. "She's having a hard time getting through to the end of the school year. Normally I have my girls make their own phone calls, but she's just too down to do anything right now."

"Her teachers have told me they've seen her withdraw, and that she's not herself," he said. "I've seen it myself, as she's worked with the school on some of her performances. Normally she's such a pleasant and happy young woman. I've seen a real difference."

"You know," I said, "when she first played the harp, we rented one and brought it home. You're supposed to play an hour a day at first, to build up your calluses. Well, she came to me after playing for five hours straight—her fingers were bleeding, and she was sobbing, just sobbing, that she'd figured out how to play this Joanna Newsom song already. She was so happy about it. I knew right then that she'd found a passion. She was in love with this instrument. She's even pursued it as a career now, which is incredible." My voice broke, and I struggled to continue. "Now, she doesn't even want to touch it. The harp is sitting there, and she has no desire to go near it—she's too depressed. It's heartbreaking."

"I'm so sorry to hear it," he said. We talked some more, and he said that they would be able to hold her scholarship, provided she could keep her 3.0 cumulative GPA.

That was going to be the real feat. She'd struggled all semester, to the point where she was unable to do anything in her classes. She was completely behind in all of them.

In working with her teachers, we figured out ways to pull her through, including changing most of her classes to pass/fail. I was grateful for their understanding and willingness to work with her. Although she did ultimately fail one class, her prior GPA was enough to keep her above the required 3.0.

Now we'd cleared some hurdles, at least. The scholarship would be ready and waiting when she felt well enough to return. I had to believe she would.

Jane and I sat together on the couch.

"You need to focus on yourself, number one," I told her. "Make sure you're healthy. Then you can decide if you should return to school. If you don't want to finish your degree, I'm okay with that—as long as you're happy. You may find that your passion for the harp comes back. Or maybe it doesn't. Either way, it's up to you. It's your life and your decision."

"I'll keep that door open in case I want to pursue it again," she said.

I paused. "But I want to ask you something."

"What is it?"

"When you went into the crisis center this time . . ." I held her hand and hesitated, unsure if I should continue. "I overheard you telling them on the phone that you'd written goodbye letters."

Jane's bright-blue eyes found mine. "Yes, I did."

"Who did you write them to?"

"Friends, family, my sisters—people I care about."

"Did you write one to me?" I asked.

"Yes, of course."

"What did you say?"

"I told you I loved you. I said I didn't want to say goodbye."

My voice broke. "Then why would you leave us, Jane? If you don't want to? I don't understand."

"Because, Mom, I'm in pain, every day. It hurts to be alive. I don't want to leave you, or anyone else, but the pain is unbearable. I literally hurt everywhere, emotionally and physically. Every day is agony. I feel like I can't take it anymore. I'm suffering."

"I'm so sorry for what you're going through." I hugged her as tears slid down my face. "It's so hard to see you hurting. We'll do whatever it takes to get you some help. But please, please promise me you'll at least try to get better."

"I will try. I promise," she said. "I do want to get better. I do! I don't want to die."

We held each other and cried together. I prayed for some relief for her through her medications or therapy. I had some hope knowing that, unlike Noel at the time, she didn't actually *want* to die. But we had to deal with the hopelessness she felt.

# TURNING POINT

Over the next two months, Jane dutifully sat for her three-hour dialectical behavior therapy (DBT) sessions multiple times a week. Eventually, she started to speak more positively and with more hope.

"You know," she said, "I'm learning how to think differently. They're showing us ways to respond to different emotional triggers."

"That's so encouraging," I said, feeling relieved that something finally seemed to be working.

"I used to think I had to suffer through my emotions," she said. "I thought there was nothing I could do to stop them. They would take over my whole body, flooding me, and I thought that's just the way it had to be. Now I know how to take control of them. I feel a lot better."

Dialectical behavior therapy focuses on ways to improve emotion regulation, interpersonal skills, and distress tolerance, and it also teaches mindfulness. It's been proven to be highly effective in curtailing suicidal ideation.

After five weeks of group DBT sessions, Jane told me, "This has changed my life. We journal, and I get to share in this group of people who understand what I'm going through. And everyone is telling me that my willingness to share so openly encourages them to do the same."

We sat for an hour as she enthusiastically showed me the hundred-page book that accompanied the course. It was filled with step-by-step instructions on how to approach different problems.

I could see that this type of program was a good fit for her personality.

"This is amazing," I said. "Do you feel more confident now about how you can cope with things in the future?"

"Yes, I do—I'm so happy," she said. "I feel so much better now and hopeful." She leaned in to hug me.

Once again, I was amazed by how professional help can change a situation from reactive to proactive, from self-destructive to beneficial.

Once again, we'd found a way out of the darkness.

I marvel at the power of knowledge to change things, even in the direst circumstances. After she learned the causes of her PTSD, Jane was able to stop bottling up her pain—by using the skills she learned in the DBT program to deal with the emotions that used to control her.

DBT gave her hope. What more could a mother ask for? If she has that, she has everything ... and her future will be hers for the taking.

# ROSE

Supporting a suicidal child affects your whole family. Period. There's no getting around it.

It takes a toll on siblings to see each other struggle. There's a lot of stress in the house, and their brother or sister may be angry or behaving recklessly. This is frightening to watch, and it may make siblings feel unsafe or insecure. Nothing seems to make sense like it used to. The family is turned upside down.

A lot of time, energy, and emotion goes into all of this—it's incredibly exhausting. As parents, our energy may not go toward the ones who are doing okay for the moment. We simply lack the bandwidth.

Beware.

Don't assume that if they say nothing, they're all right.

My family learned this the hard way.

When Rose was born, her sisters were absolutely delighted to be gifted with this little treasure. She was like a living doll to them. They fawned over her and loved to make funny faces to make her laugh.

As she grew, Rose looked up to her sisters. She wanted to be where they were, do what they were doing. Jane and Noel, five and three at the time, twirled around in their princess dresses and sang a much-loved song they'd memorized from one of the Barbie movies they loved to watch.

Rose, just two, spun around with them in her Cinderella dress. The three of them together were such a happy little trio.

How carefree they were back then.

For years, Rose watched wide-eyed as her sisters' emotional states transformed from normal to extreme. She witnessed the rages they unleashed on everyone around them. She heard them repeatedly threaten to kill themselves. Over the next few years, she lived in constant fear of it possibly happening.

Rose saw her sisters perched on the edge of suicide. She absorbed everything—the panicked moments where she was ushered to the neighbors' house to wait in fear as her sister was driven to the ER, her parents' stress, and the potential death of one or both of her siblings. It all became bewildering and terrifying.

Rose internalized the stress that permeated our once-peaceful home. Now, at fifteen, she began to withdraw, spending more time in her room.

One Saturday afternoon, I realized I hadn't seen Rose all day. I went to her room to check on her. She was lying in bed, her arm flung over her eyes. She peeked out at me as I came in.

"Are you still in bed? Or just taking a nap?" I asked.

"I haven't gotten up yet," she said.

"It's three o'clock! Were you up late or something?"

"No, I can't get up. I don't have any energy."

I put my hand on her forehead. "You don't feel warm. Are you feeling sick?"

"No, I just feel like I can't move."

My concern began to grow. I perched beside her on the edge of her bed.

"What's going on?" I asked.

"I'm feeling really sad. Depressed," she said, tears leaking from the corners of her eyes.

"Oh, no, I'm so sorry!" I stroked her hair. "What can I do to help you?"

"Nothing. I don't know. I just feel so overwhelmed right now. I can't handle anything. I'm just so sad all the time. I don't care about anything."

"How bad is it? Can you tell me?" I asked, holding my breath.

We'd both been down this road before. She knew what I was asking.

"I'm thinking about suicide."

My heart stopped. *Oh my god. No!*

"Are you planning to do something to hurt yourself? You have to tell me!"

"No, but I'm having thoughts about it."

*How can this be . . . again? How? My poor girl!*

Rose had never said a word about feeling this poorly; I never knew. What a shock to find out that, in attending to all the other crises for the other two, the third had gone down. I was so not prepared for this. Blindsided . . . again.

"Please, you have to promise me you won't do anything," I said. "We're going to get you help. Let's get you some counseling and start working on this, okay?"

"Okay," she said and shrugged, despondent. Tears streamed onto her pillow.

"You can get better! Don't give up. Will you promise me to at least try?"

She stared up at the ceiling as her tears continued. She was silent.

"Please!" I implored. "Please just tell me that you'll try to get better."

She regarded me steadily, her dark-blue eyes locking onto mine.

"Okay, I will," she finally said.

I released my breath and put my head down onto her shoulder as I hugged her.

I had learned from experience by now: I knew not to let this sit and fester. I had a clear sense of déjà vu as I picked up the phone and dialed the number for a therapist.

# TERRIFIED

Rose started working with a therapist. With her permission, I sat in on one of her early therapy sessions.

The therapist pulled out a bunch of cards at random and put them on the floor. They were all short phrases describing how someone might be feeling. Rose was asked to pick out the ones that best fit her emotions. She chose four or five of the cards.

After talking things through a bit more, the therapist asked her to pare it down to the one most pressing emotion. Rose chose one card and moved it to the top of the array. It read: *I don't feel safe*.

My first response was puzzlement. We had a safe home, didn't we? But then I thought about it again. Maybe not. Growing up, her father lost his temper a lot—to the point where we weren't sure what could happen. That created a lot of anxiety for all of us.

And her sisters' safety had been in doubt for the past few years. There was no way she couldn't have been affected by everything that had transpired around her.

With a suicidal person in the house, everything has the potential to become a life-or-death situation. You're always wondering what else could happen. Will they do it again? No matter what you do to keep them safe, they could still run in front of a car, jump off a bridge. The possibility becomes a constant, underlying source of stress for everyone. The fear stays with you.

These revelations helped me understand how Rose had come to feel suicidal. Rose has a naturally anxious personality, and after years of uncertainty in her home environment, her anxiety levels had increased to the point where it affected her ability to cope.

Her state of stress began to come out in the form of panic attacks. She came to my room late one night and said, "Mom, I think I'm having a stroke."

I sat up in bed. "What? Why? What's going on?"

"I'm having trouble breathing, and my eyes are blurry."

"Are you sure you aren't just tired? Why don't we look it up?" After finding the list of symptoms online and talking it over, she knew she wasn't having a stroke after all.

"Do you think this could be anxiety?" I asked. "Remember how we talked with your therapist? You told her you were afraid you were going to die."

"Yeah, you're right. I know what you're saying."

After some reassurance and back rubs, she was feeling better and headed off to bed.

Other times, she was short of breath. "I feel like I can't breathe. I can't catch my breath."

"Remember when we did all those tests and the doctor said everything is fine—that you're really healthy?" I said. "And he said the more you think about not being able to breathe, the more you won't be able to breathe? This happened to me one time when I was stuck in a stairwell. By the time I was able to figure out where the exit was, I was panting and sweating and couldn't breathe. The mind and body are totally connected to each other."

Other times, it was mysterious lumps in the throat, random stomachaches, and a sudden, irrational feeling that she might have Lyme disease. For her, anxiety reappeared as hypochondria.

As Rose continued with her therapist, she processed past events and her responses to them. She learned to put things in perspective and live in the moment. She found ways to de-stress. She relearned to breathe without thinking about it.

Through this work with her therapist, she was able to let go of feeling responsible for others' behavior. She began focusing on herself—but in a much healthier way. She discovered her innate need to be the "perfect" child to make life less stressful for me and her sisters. It's what she learned to do early on. She saw how hard this was on all of us, so she tried her best to make things easier. She would often sweep up or do the dishes, never complaining about anything. She had become self-effacing, erasing herself as she shrank out of sight.

She learned to speak up for herself when she didn't agree with something. She no longer let herself get railroaded into what she didn't want to do. She learned to have boundaries.

She also started to acknowledge what affected her state of mind.

"Rose," I asked her, "do you remember some of the things that happened in our house when you were younger?"

I listed a few incidents that stood out to me for their chaos and volatility.

"You know, Mom, as I'm talking to my therapist, I'm realizing that I don't remember some of the things Jane and Noel do. I think I'm repressing a lot of memories."

"Maybe it's a way for you to protect yourself? Because you don't want to remember?"

"I think that's it," she said. "I think it's my way of dealing with things."

Rose told me a story of when she was little, about her father calling for her from upstairs. She didn't hear him, so she didn't respond.

He came down the stairs and started yelling at her.

"Why don't you answer me when I call for you? And why are these princess dresses all over the floor?" he screamed. "It's such a mess in here!"

She started to cry. Her father then sat on the floor, picked up a nearby mask, and put it on. He started to laugh and be silly and make funny faces. Rose continued crying.

"What's wrong?" he asked her, as if nothing had happened.

The familiar sadness came to me. *It never ends. We think it's over, but it isn't.*

An incident like this might seem benign, like no big deal. But when it happens over and over, it's hurtful. It's depressing. Getting yelled at repeatedly is traumatizing. Rose did nothing to deserve it.

I also feel sad for her father, whose actions alienated him from his daughters over time. Despite my anger over his behavior, I pity him. He battles his own demons. But ultimately, our family suffered for it.

"I should have left the marriage sooner," I told her, tears filling my eyes. "You were just little girls having to deal with all this. I feel so guilty. I'm so sorry. I feel like I could have done something. It was up to me to protect you."

"Mom," Rose said, taking my hand and squeezing it tightly, "please don't blame yourself. You helped us."

"How?"

"You listened. You were there for us. You've always been there for us. You inspired us to fight to get better," she said, hugging me.

I squeezed my eyes shut and fought against the sobs that threatened to overtake me.

"You are such an amazing girl. You're so understanding and kind."

"You know," she said, "I think I might like to be a counselor someday. I'd really like to help others."

"Really? That's awesome! I bet you'd be so good at it."

"Maybe I could be a writer too? I'm not sure."

"You don't have to figure it out today," I said. "But doesn't it feel good to know you have so many choices ahead of you? It's pretty exciting."

"It is," she agreed.

Through therapy, thankfully, the pull of suicide receded from Rose's mind. Once again, I was thankful for the intervention of a professional who opened her eyes to other ways to process how she was feeling. It made all the difference in helping her find her strength once again. My heart rejoiced to see it.

# READY TO FLY

A few months after Jane's second trip to the crisis center, I sat on the front porch. It was a gorgeous summer night, and the golden, late-day sun filtered through the leaves as I enjoyed the pleasant warmth of the evening.

Soothing wisps of music from Jane's harp floated into the night. I was overjoyed to hear that sound again. It was the sound of healing.

She'd started writing music in earnest again, practicing on the harp and strumming her guitar as she tried different lines. It had been a long time since she'd played any instruments or brought forth her lovely voice. Now, her passion for music was reawakening.

Noel came running down the street, back from a jog. She ran up the front steps and sat next to me.

"I beat my time on my running record today," she said.

"How cool! You're really loving running, aren't you?"

"It makes me feel amazing—it's a way for me to work out my problems. I think it has a lot to do with why I'm feeling so much better now." She paused to take a drink from her water bottle. "Hey, I have some exciting news."

"What is it?"

"I had my last psychiatrist appointment today. She says I don't have to go back anymore. I'm done."

"Really? That's incredible!"

"She said I'm doing so well off the meds that she doesn't think I'll ever need them again. She says I'm doing awesome."

"Noel, that's wonderful. Look at where you were just a few years ago, and look at where you are now. You've come so far. You amaze me, honestly."

"Aw. Thank you, Mama." She gave me a hug, then hesitated. "But it seems like you still want to bring up the past a lot. I don't really feel like talking about it anymore. Does that make sense? I want to focus on what's ahead of me now, not what I've left behind."

"I know. It was a traumatic time for all of us, though, and for me as your mother. Plus, I still worry about Jane and Rose. They're still struggling a bit and figuring things out. I guess I need to talk about it because I still have some healing to do. I think sharing with others is my way of processing everything."

"I get it," she said. "That's okay. Everyone's different. I'm just at the point now where I want to move on."

"Totally understandable," I said.

"Also, you know how Greer and I have been looking for apartments? Well, there's one place we really love. I think we're going to put a deposit on it to hold it for August."

"Wow, that's so cool!" I said. Greer was one of Noel's best friends and now roommate-to-be. "I'll be honest, though, I'm going to miss you... and your cooking."

We laughed. Noel had become a talented cook, and she made meals for the family several times a week.

"I'm sad to be leaving home," she said. "But I'm excited to have my own place."

"Hey, when I was eighteen, I couldn't wait to move out. It's a normal thing," I said.

*She's ready to fly.*

"I'm going to shower before Greer gets here. We're going to the drive-in," Noel said.

As she opened the front door, I heard Jane and Rose laughing inside the house as Rose played "Clair de Lune" on the piano.

A few minutes later, Jane came out on the porch carrying the blanket she was crocheting. "Look, I'm almost done!" she said.

She'd been making it for her aunt, my sister, who was going through cancer treatments. She'd put countless hours into its creation. It had been a therapeutic outlet for her as she had begun facing her issues and finding better ways to deal with them.

"I'm so glad you made this for Aunt Gail," I said. "I know she'll love it. I'm so excited for her to see it!"

"I love it so much. I think she's going to be happy to get it. It makes me feel good to do this for her."

Jane had been back at home for a few months after her last visit to the crisis center. Now she was ready to return home.

I was sad to see her go. It had been a while since she'd lived at home, and it was wonderful to have her back with us again. But she wanted to get back to her apartment, her friends, and her own life.

Jane and I sat together quietly for a while as she put the finishing touches on the blanket.

A car pulled up: Noel's roommate-to-be. Noel came out of the house, hair still wet from her shower.

"I'll see you later, sis," she said to Jane, hugging her. "Good luck with everything."

"Love you, sissie," Jane called out as Noel jumped in the car and zoomed off.

Jane finished the blanket, and we found a box that it fit in so I could mail it to her aunt in the morning.

Rose came out on the porch.

"You're going back home tonight then?" she asked Jane.

"Yeah," said Jane. "Time to get back to work and all that good stuff."

"I'll miss you," Rose said and hugged her. "I love you."

"I love you, and I'll miss you too, sissie," Jane said. "I'll call you."

I helped Jane pack her car and stood with her in the driveway. We talked for a long time, both reluctant to say goodbye.

"I'm feeling so much better," she said. "I think when I get back home, I'll start another blanket for my friend's birthday. And I have more ideas for songs I want to write."

"I think you're starting to heal," I said.

She nodded and smiled.

"I'm so proud of you, Jane," I added. "You've come so far. You've worked so hard."

"Thanks, Mom. You've done so much for me. I appreciate everything."

"Of course," I said. "That's what mothers do."

We smiled and stood silently in the driveway for a moment.

"I love you, angel."

"I love you too, Mom."

"Make good choices and remember—I'm always here."

"I know. Thank you so much. I can't say it enough."

She got in the car and started to drive away. I stood in the driveway, waving wildly and blowing her kisses. A surge of hope and love for my girl filled my heart.

"I love you!" I called out as tears rolled down my cheeks.

"Bye, sis! Love you!" Rose called from the front porch.

"Bye! Love you guys!" Jane shouted from the car window as she drove away, back to her own life and independence once again.

*She's off and running. A little more ready to take on the world.*

I stood for a moment more, regaining my composure before returning to the porch.

Two of my birds were taking flight, but Rose was still with me in the nest.

"Well, Rose," I said, wrapping my arm around her shoulder, "it looks like it's you and me. Why don't we listen to some music? How 'bout we put our jammies on and take turns sharing songs we like on Spotify?"

"Great!" she said.

"I want to go first, though, okay?" I said.

"Sure."

My darling little rosebud. Always in the moment, always up for anything. Always easygoing and sweet.

We went off to change into comfy clothes, and then we sat side by side on the couch.

"It's called 'Blackbird.' It's by the Beatles," I told her. We huddled together as we listened.

"Ooh, I like it," Rose said.

"Me too." I closed my eyes for a moment and breathed deeply. *I think we're going to be all right.*

A profound sense of peace filled me. It had been years since I'd felt this way.

"Mom, I was wondering if you could teach me how to sew this summer," Rose said. "I think that'd be fun."

"Sure, let's do it! Why don't I teach you how to use my old camera too? We can take pictures and videos with it. I'm up for anything. We'll have a blast this summer—no matter what. How does that sound?"

"Sounds amazing! Love you, Mom."

"Love you more."

The harrowing times we've been through have bonded us; now we're cemented and strong. Together, we've healed.

Today, Rose, Noel, Jane, and I continue on our journey to healing. We stand ready to move forward to better days. The future belongs to us once again, and we'll never take each other for granted.

After the darkest, most helpless of nights, we approach a hopeful dawn—a new chapter for our family. I'm grateful we've found our way.

Good or bad, we will cherish every moment of our lives. Each one is a gift.

*Thank you, God.*

# Part Two

## LOOKING AHEAD

# PART TWO: LOOKING AHEAD

The battle with depression has left scars on my girls that I'm not sure will ever leave them. They'll always carry the pain with them at some level. But maybe that's not all bad; after all, their ordeals have shaped them into the compassionate, tenacious, and strong young women they are today.

Here, they share the lessons they learned and explain what's helped them survive.

These girls are amazing. I'm so proud to be their mom.

# RISING ABOVE

*By Jane*

My heart goes out to anyone battling with the tricky animal of trauma—it's much more common than people think. I would argue that everyone in the world has experienced some level of trauma, whether it came from being bullied as a kid or going through a hard breakup.

Every time I've felt suicidal, I've been in a lot of emotional pain. I think suicidality is born out of the feeling that you'll never be able to escape that pain.

I looked to nature to help myself. I went out of my way to go hiking and camping, and I also paid attention to nature in my everyday life. The leaves on the trees fall one by one; the landscape of the clouds is different every hour.

I believe everything is constantly changing in endless, intricate ways—including the hills and valleys of your own psyche and those of every person around you. Everything in the world has a rise and fall that's born of the constant dance between the forces of life and death present everywhere, drawn out over time. Even the mountains are painstakingly resculpting themselves.

I've felt this cycle within myself as I transform through experiencing new things. An acceptance of the presence of death in life is important when processing trauma. Everything eventually withers over time, and so will your pain after a traumatic event.

Reliving your memories is a natural part of processing trauma. It's painful, but it functions like a physical healing process, like exercising a wounded muscle. Your psyche wants to heal, and the traumatic memories feel gradually less painful over time.

Something I've observed in myself is my tendency to "overexercise" my trauma, thinking about it obsessively and spiraling as a result. Many of my suicidal episodes have come from this pattern. However, it's also problematic to repress your trauma entirely.

For better or worse, we all have to live with every experience we have. You won't be able to hide from your trauma, so it's best to find the balance between these unhealthy extremes—letting yourself feel the pain necessary to process what happened while being gentle with yourself.

I encourage you to do everything you can to endure the pain of processing trauma because you can count on the fact that your thoughts and emotions will change over time.

At my lowest points in dealing with my trauma, I always turn to music. I'm in awe of how I see different parts of myself reflected in other people's music, and for this reason, listening to music is often a cathartic experience.

When I was in so much emotional pain that it felt like my body was on fire, the harsh noise, heavy guitars, and dark, yelled lyrics of Death Grips' songs felt like they were saving my life. Listening to them was like hearing my unbearable inner feelings reflected back to me, which was such a comfort.

After I started writing music again, I found emotional stability for what felt like the first time in my life. It was like I was less stuck inside myself, like my overpowering, self-contained feelings finally had somewhere to go. I think this is true of any form of self-expression, be it something formal like visual art, film, or writing, or something as everyday as the way you dress or decorate your living space. It's empowering to be able to externalize emotions.

I believe self-expression is a beautiful tool for self-discovery. When you're trying to heal from trauma, try to do something that expresses who you are. Try painting something in watercolor or rearranging your room, then see what parts of yourself are reflected in what you're doing. I think the best defense possible against trauma is having a strong relationship with and understanding of yourself. If you're comfortable with yourself, you'll make it through anything.

# ON THE OTHER SIDE

*By Noel*

As a teenager who's dealt with the unbearable disease of depression for years, I can say that feeling suicidal isn't something you can truly understand without experiencing it firsthand.

Watching a loved one go through it can provide a glimpse into the mind of someone who wants to end their life, but there's no formula to suicidal thoughts and tendencies. You never know what's going on in someone's life, and a person can feel this way for any reason or no reason at all.

We can study these tendencies using science and brain chemicals to explain the process, but in my opinion, the important thing to understand is that feeling like your life isn't worth living anymore sucks. That's really the most accurate word for it.

When you feel like you shouldn't be around anymore, you lose your will to do anything because you feel like nothing matters. You stop caring about your relationships with people because you believe it's better to distance yourself—you're actively imagining yourself being gone.

You don't care about your future because you genuinely don't think you have one. This strips you of your will to contribute positively to anything, and you end up spiraling. At least, that was my experience.

Most of my high school classmates have endured periods of depression, and many have had suicidal tendencies as well. I often ask myself how it's possible that our society enables, ignores, and creates so much pain and depression in teens—it's to the point where almost everyone I know has been affected by it.

The students at my public school come from different backgrounds and home lives to begin with, and then we're expected to conform to our given genders and ideals and forms of femininity or masculinity. We feel pressured to impress our crushes, to be what the kids who get attention want us to be. We search for the emotional aspects we're missing at home or within ourselves in people who don't have our best interests in mind.

This was all exhausting for me, and it made my suicidal times even more difficult—especially because the core reasons for my suicidal thoughts had to do with these kinds of pressures and issues. The feeling of something always seeming off, and the heaviness that came along with it, only seemed to grow and grow.

During the rockiest part of my mental health journey, I slowly came to realize that so many things we expect to be fair just aren't. For example, when I thought about the financial aspect of my first hospitalization early on, my chest panged with guilt. Why did we need to pay for and worry about mental health crisis bills in the middle of a mental health crisis across society? This made it more difficult for me to accept the situation and begin the healing process. Instead, I turned to anger and carelessness to cope.

Unfortunately, there are reminders everywhere that life is difficult and hurtful. But I've found that optimism is the best way to get through it.

I've also found exercise to be a great way to train myself to deal with tough situations. When I push myself in a workout or run to the point where I want to give up more than anything, I keep going instead. I'm practicing being there for myself.

Exercising has built up my confidence in myself mentally. I know that when I want to give up in other unpleasant situations, emotionally or otherwise, I can get myself through it. Over time, this has made me better at coping with shaky circumstances that would've been overwhelming for me a few years ago.

Exercise has tons of physical and mental health benefits, and in my eyes, challenging yourself always builds character and confidence. You're doing your best for yourself and putting work into yourself, even if you feel like you're not worth it at first.

You're teaching yourself that you deserve to be well, and that spreads into all aspects of your life.

# GRATEFUL

*By Rose*

Something my mom tells me and my sisters a lot is how sad it makes her that she stayed with my dad for as long as she did. Their divorce eventually brought on a wave of peace as the tension eased and our environment became healthier, but the trauma of our early household stuck with us, and we all ended up suffering in different ways because of it.

My mom often says she wishes she'd left sooner, to lessen the damage those years inflicted on us.

"It's hard enough to leave a traumatic situation, even without kids," we always tell her.

But no amount of reassurance, healing, or perspective seems to ease her guilt. Mom suffered a lot of damage from those years and the future they inflicted. Not only has she had to face her own traumas and anxieties, but she's also seen the inevitable effect those years had on us.

She still feels the aftershock of "if only I'd done something sooner"—the type that's often countered with, "You can't change the past. You can only control what happens next."

The idea that we can't change the past is true and easy to understand. But it's often hard to believe. How can someone just accept these horrible experiences they or their loved ones had to go through when—with one little nudge of fate or intent—they could have been avoided?

We say wishfully, "If I'd just known sooner." "If I hadn't ignored it."

"If I'd known the damage it would do."

No matter how hard we try to be rational and self-forgiving, the what-ifs almost always have it. Of course the past is impermeable; yes, it always could have been worse. Everything always could have been better too. Faster, richer, healthier, more important.

The future is an infinite array, but the past is a single chain cutting ruthlessly into possibility. This is what we try to tell ourselves in the throes of post-trauma, but it's so hard to believe when we are waist-deep in a pool of suffering.

But despite the terror, it's hard not to wonder. Wildfires that ravage and destroy allow trees to grow back stronger later on. Could the same be said about human beings?

In a strange, twisted way, I've come to believe that trauma can bring goodness into the human experience. Of course, trauma should never be wished for, and living without it would no doubt result in an easier life with less darkness.

But nonetheless, I feel almost grateful for the way it's shaped me. I believe that being forced to pull myself back up from my lows has made me stronger. I believe being so down has awakened an empathy and emotional knowledge I never would've known otherwise.

I believe feeling such intense despair has widened the spectrum in which I can feel things like joy and love too. The way I've had to reevaluate beauty means when I find myself in it, it's brighter, more exciting, more dear to me. The joys of life are refreshing now—and harder to take for granted.

I think even little things like my humor, confidence, and passions were spurred on by trauma, and those things drew me to valuable friends I still have, who support and understand me when I find myself still down. They've been a big part of my recovery.

It's impossible not to look back, to think of the little things you could've done to avoid pain for yourself or the ones you love. I sometimes find myself wishing things had been different.

But if given the choice, I don't think I'd change anything about my past. It led me to the friends, feelings, and appreciation for life that I have now. In a way, my life is richer because of the pain I've felt. Eventually, great sorrow is always, somehow, paired with even greater joy.

# Part Three

**12 WAYS TO EMPOWER
YOUR PARENTING**

# PART THREE: 12 WAYS TO EMPOWER YOUR PARENTING

I don't know if the day will ever come when I don't feel the weight of sadness for what my family has gone through. I agonize over the pain my daughters faced. How heartbroken I am for them.

It's not surprising that, as their mother, I've felt (and sometimes still feel) depressed, guilty, angry, alone, and terrified. Of course, these are all normal responses to chaos, stress, and, ultimately, the fear of losing a precious child.

In this section, I come to you as a parent who's walked through fire. I know this is one of the toughest roads a parent can ever travel—one fraught with countless unknowns and constant fear. It feels so overwhelming that it's hard to keep going sometimes. It's hard to stay strong.

The following pages offer my advice based on what I learned through my mistakes, regrets, and failures . . . but also through my successes. There's a lot of trial and error when things are so volatile.

I'm here to offer you encouragement and support. I'm cheering you on! You can do this! Despite how difficult it can be, there's a lot you can do to empower yourself to make it through.

Follow your heart in all you do. Love will lead the way.

# FIND OUTSIDE SUPPORT

It isn't the time to be a hero and try to do this alone. You simply can't.

Reach out to professionals who know what they're doing. You'll see far better outcomes than if you try to do this alone or wait until things resolve. With no intervention, things may only worsen over time. You may find yourself regretting a decision to let it ride.

While it is helpful to seek out informational websites and books that can guide you in understanding what's going on in your child's mind (I've included some recommended resources at the back of this book), there is no one-size-fits-all solution. Each family faces unique obstacles. Trained professionals assess your situation and suggest the best possible course of action.

At one point, I participated in a parent support group, a subset of Noel's intensive therapy program. It helped to know that other parents were going through the same situation and had the same fears and doubts about themselves. The kind man who led the group helped us understand the complexity of our children's behaviors. (Many assume that suicidal thoughts and attempts only involve teens, but more young children than ever are becoming depressed and suicidal. For this reason, I will use *child* and *children* as well as *tweens* and *teens* in this section.)

Professionals know how to deal with suicidal teens; they can help facilitate short-term stabilization and long-term healing. They know what to say and do (and what not to say and do) when someone is in imminent danger. They are trained to see patterns of behavior in your child or your family that you'll never see on your own. They know how to work with your child using medication, therapy, and other treatment options. They can guide you in finding additional support in your area.

You can get help from many different types of professionals: psychiatrists, psychologists, therapists, therapeutic horseback riding centers, treatment facilities, crisis centers … we used all of these, and I'm incredibly grateful for their nonjudgmental, skilled intervention when it was desperately needed. Their support and guidance changed the trajectory of each of my daughters' lives. I'm so grateful to them.

> They are trained to see patterns of behavior in your child or your family that you'll never see on your own.

All kinds of professionals can provide a valuable role. Noel's school counselor, for example, spent time with her whenever she needed a break from her classes because of her anxiety. She helped Noel make it through the school day and cope with everything. In turn, Noel being able to attend school gave me a reprieve from the constant supervision she needed when she was at home. What a godsend!

Whatever treatment protocol you seek and whoever helps you, keep this in mind: These professionals are trained in what they do. They know how to stay calm in crisis. They've seen this all before. They're there to help and guide your child, you, and your family.

I can't emphasize enough how important it is for you to find professionals to support you in this journey. Don't wait a day longer if you're hesitant to reach out for help. Listen to your intuition. It can be the difference between life and death.

You need all the help you can get right now—don't face this alone.

## EMPOWERED PARENTING AFFIRMATION

I'm not alone in facing this. I can reach out to others who are willing to help.

## SELF-REFLECTION

Make a list of professional support systems you've tried so far.

What else can you take advantage of?

What other supports exist in your community?

## LET IT GO

Being on suicide watch is extremely chaotic and emotional—stress rules your life. Running around to this, that, and the other event, lesson, or meeting on top of it doesn't help.

Pare down stressors by deciding what's essential and what isn't. The key to staying afloat during this time is to ask yourself, "What can I let go of right now?"

For example, how can you streamline daily chores or meals? Who can come over and give you a break? Find ways to make things easier.

> The key to staying afloat during this time is to ask yourself, "What can I let go of right now?"

I started freezer cooking once a month with a great friend. We played the radio and talked, and the day's labor yielded a month's worth of freezer meals. After long, stressful days, the family was able to eat a good meal with little effort.

Also, keep in mind that letting go has to do with emotional baggage too. You know what weighs us down the most? Guilt. It's a terrible beast that nags at us and sows doubt. We start to second-guess the decisions we made. We feel like we should've seen the signs. Doubts creep in. We believe we've mishandled the situation. We beat ourselves up for what we should've or could've done.

Guilt is a form of grief; it's regret for what didn't happen. We're grieving the loss of what could have been.

We're grieving the inability to prevent our child's suffering.

Please be kind to yourself. You can't change the past, and you can't change what's happened. You can only do your best in the days to come.

Let it go, and move forward in the most positive direction you possibly can.

# EMPOWERED PARENTING AFFIRMATION

I allow myself to release what weighs me down.

## SELF-REFLECTION

What guilt or regret are you holding on to when it comes to your current situation?

_____
_____
_____
_____

How can you be kinder to yourself and give yourself grace?

_____
_____
_____

On the next few pages, spend some time recording different stressors, and put one or more check marks next to who's most affected by it—you, your child, or your family. List the action steps you can take to address each situation. Choose a few to start working on. Make a plan, and stick to it!

| STRESSOR | ■ Me |
| | ■ Child |
| | ■ Family |

**ACTIONS**

---

| STRESSOR | ■ Me |
| | ■ Child |
| | ■ Family |

**ACTIONS**

---

| STRESSOR | ■ Me |
| | ■ Child |
| | ■ Family |

**ACTIONS**

| STRESSOR | ☐ Me ☐ Child ☐ Family |
|---|---|

**ACTIONS**

| STRESSOR | ☐ Me ☐ Child ☐ Family |
|---|---|

**ACTIONS**

| STRESSOR | ☐ Me ☐ Child ☐ Family |
|---|---|

**ACTIONS**

| STRESSOR | | Me |
| | | Child |
| | | Family |

**ACTIONS**

| STRESSOR | | Me |
| | | Child |
| | | Family |

**ACTIONS**

| STRESSOR | | Me |
| | | Child |
| | | Family |

**ACTIONS**

# REDUCE SCREEN TIME

The online realm has created huge stress for our children. The world is in the palm of their hands. These little devices can create wonderful connections to others, but they also broadcast countless, constant problems: there's an earthquake in Nepal, a murder in Dallas, a bombing in a nearby town. Humans—and especially children—aren't wired to be bombarded by this massive amount of negativity.

Add to this the pressure to keep up one's online image. Apps transform us into more beautiful versions of ourselves. Teens count and compare the number of "likes" they get on their photos. When their self-esteem is tied to the online world, it can become an unhealthy obsession that adds stress and causes depression.

> Humans—and especially children—aren't wired to be bombarded by this massive amount of negativity.

When I was a teacher, I believed that my main mission, besides educating, was to build self-esteem. A child with strong self-esteem is more likely to achieve their goals and stay emotionally robust.

Children will defy the odds if they believe they can do something—and if the people they care about believe they can too. The online world is filled with phonies and haters. Are they who your child needs? The people your child encounters in day-to-day life—not online—are far more likely to be supporters.

The online world has also become a place that breeds bullying. Online, children (and just as many adults) are emboldened to say things they would never say to someone's face. I call this the *snipe-and-hide* mentality. Online, anyone can be mean, and no one faces any real consequences. And when a child is invited to share too much or makes a poor decision to post or message something they later regret, shame pours fuel on the fire—especially if they're already feeling suicidal.

What can you do when your child is suicidal? First, turn off the news and don't talk about the problems in the world. Then, limit your child's phone use while encouraging healthier in-person interactions with friends and family members.

Why not take away their phone entirely? Well, even though it can add to their stress, almost all children communicate with their friends this way. If you take their phone away entirely in hopes of removing negative influences, you'll also be removing part of their support system.

Teens, in particular, feel a strong need to belong. That can't happen when they're yanked from the ability to communicate the way they're used to. The professionals we dealt with in our journey said the same thing: you can take away the phone entirely, but that will just drive it all underground. Eventually, kids have to learn what creates toxicity and what creates well-being—and how to make better choices for themselves.

So, aim to limit screen time and help your child establish healthier patterns.

# EMPOWERED PARENTING AFFIRMATION

I will stay open to the awareness of what outside influences are affecting my children and my family.

## SELF-REFLECTION

How do you feel about the amount of time your family spends on screens?

___

How do you think screen exposure is affecting your family?

___

Do you know what your child is really doing online and where they're spending the most time? What do you think they're doing?

___

Have a conversation with your child about what's going on in their online life and how it may be affecting them. Share how it went.

___

Find two ways to lessen screen time in your house (for example, putting phones away at a certain time and not allowing phones at dinner) and implement them.

___

# TAKE CARE OF YOURSELF

As a parent, I also battled the terrifying pull of depression. I fell into a pit of emotional concrete that sucked me down and set around me. My despondency paralyzed me, rendered me helpless, and beat every bit of energy from my body and soul. Some days, I couldn't move my legs to get out of bed.

During one of my worst lows, my friend called me, and we went on a two-mile walk. For the first time in my life, I experienced a "runner's high"—a rushing, euphoric feeling. It was

> You need to charge your batteries now and then so you can keep going.

my body's response to the serotonin released by exercising. Because I'd been so physically and emotionally depressed, the exercise had created an intense counter-response.

*Wow, I should exercise more*, I thought. This one simple, natural thing could make me feel so much better. It was something I could do for myself. It was one way to relieve the stress.

It's draining to go through these emotional roller coasters over and over. It demands a lot of your energy. You need to charge your batteries now and then so you can keep going.

Do a puzzle, soak in the tub, practice yoga or meditation, watch an uplifting movie, take a drive, call a friend ... do anything to give your mind a rest.

In the midst of my family's chaos, I started to take singing lessons.

I'm not an exceptional singer, but it's something I love to do. I sing all the time, belting out snippets of songs from the past—sad songs, soulful songs, joyful songs. Singing fills my heart. Taking lessons was something I could do for myself that brought joy.

Find something joyful you can latch on to! Anywhere you can find a moment of happiness will uplift you and give you a sense of normalcy and peace amid the chaos.

It may feel like you can't fit in one more thing right now because everything you do revolves around keeping your child alive. It's unbelievably exhausting. But that's even more reason to take care of yourself. If you burn yourself out or have a nervous breakdown, you won't be able to support your child. It's critical to care for yourself as well.

## EMPOWERED PARENTING AFFIRMATION

I am worthy of love and self-care. Taking care of myself will make me stronger and better able to help my family.

## SELF-REFLECTION

What do you do for yourself? What's holding you back from taking better care of yourself?

_____

_____

_____

_____

Make a list of the things you could do to relieve stress or feel better. Then, make a plan to incorporate these into your life on a regular basis.

_____

_____

_____

_____

_____

## AVOID UNSYMPATHETIC JUDGERS

Who supports you, and who brings you down? Who judges you, and who doesn't? Who stays positive, and who projects gloom and doom? Be selective in who you allow in your circle right now. The right people make all the difference in helping you stay afloat.

The key to this is to find friends who will let you speak freely without judgment. Avoid anyone who judges you, your parenting, or, above all, your child.

I attended a fundraiser a few years ago for a nonprofit that supports abused women and children. Throughout the event, we listened to speakers who were victims of abuse and watched informational videos. The audience learned about all the tactics abusers use to exert power over their victims in their efforts to control them.

> Be selective in who you allow in your circle right now. The right people make all the difference in helping you stay afloat.

When the event was over, I turned to an acquaintance I'd known for several years.

"It's hard for me to attend these events," I said. "It's triggering for me."

"What do you mean?" she asked.

"Well, there was a lot of yelling in my house. A lot of anger. We never knew when it was going to happen. It created a lot of anxiety for my girls, and it's been hard on us all. It's just been traumatizing, you know?"

"Did he ever physically abuse you? I mean, did you ever get a black eye or anything?" she asked.

> When you're going through a hard time and you share it, not everyone knows how to respond.

"No, it was all emotional and verbal. But it really affected me. I shook all the time—I felt weak, like Jell-O. And it was hard on the girls emotionally, like I said. They've all been suicidal," I said, trying not to cry.

"Well, it's not as bad as that woman who spoke today and had all those bruises and everything. You should feel lucky it wasn't as terrible as that," she said.

Her words stung like a harsh slap in the face. I reeled from the shock of her unexpected dismissiveness. I knew many people suffered at the hands of abusers, to the point of violence and even death. But that didn't mean what we went through wasn't traumatic. It was unfair to compare our situation to any other.

After this experience with my acquaintance, I began to carefully pick and choose what I would share and with whom. Obviously, not everyone would understand or offer kindness, even if it was what I needed most during our family's toughest times.

When you're going through a hard time and you share it, not everyone knows how to respond. It makes them uncomfortable. Some will back away from you in a "that's too much information" reaction. It's normal, but it's still hurtful. Be sure you trust the person with whom you share your troubles.

No matter how amazing you are as a parent, if your child is suicidal, some people will judge your parenting skills. Be prepared for it. You or your family may be the source of gossip, but it's your family, your business, and your child's life.

Some may say your child is selfish for wanting to die. I encountered this, and it was hard for me to hear. It's an incredibly hurtful statement, and it's not true. It shows a complete lack of understanding of mental illness—of the despondent state of mind that makes your child believe they'll never feel well again. It's a criticism of your child's behaviors at their lowest point. It's a criticism of your parenting too, suggesting you raised a selfish child. It's not helpful in any way.

I'm still shocked to think about how often people minimized our traumatic experiences.

"I went through the same thing, and I'm all right. It's really not such a big deal."

Or, "Noel must be overly sensitive."

> You or your family may be the source of gossip, but it's your family, your business, and your child's life.

Or, "Jane should've never invited that boy over. What did she expect?"

Where is the understanding? The compassion? If something affects a child to the point of trauma, shouldn't they be given the benefit of the doubt? Why do some so readily dismiss others' emotional struggles?

Many people don't understand mental illness. They don't understand that no, sometimes you can't just "get over it." Or they think the child is being melodramatic. Or their attitude just stinks. Or they need to just look at the bright side.

But remember this: the people who judge you certainly haven't walked in your child's shoes. Nor have they walked in yours.

In the midst of my family's struggles, judgment only pushed us down further.

> You don't need the added stress of others' judgment or ignorance.

So, stay aware of the comments people make and their insinuations. What are they really saying to you? Are they acting as judges or as supporters? Someone who sounds kind and helpful in their tone may still be hurting you with the underlying meaning or insinuation behind their words.

Listen to your own internal responses to others' comments. You know when you're feeling supported and when you're feeling judged.

Your feelings deserve to be respected. You can speak up, stand your ground, and defend yourself and your child. There's nothing wrong with asserting yourself and pointing out that these comments do nothing to help you in this moment and aren't what you need right now.

If you confront the judger and they refuse to stop the hurtful commentary, you can choose to step aside from that person. You don't need the added stress of others' judgment or ignorance.

You can agonize over the pain and damage these comments bring, or you can choose to let it go. Whatever you do, work to eliminate any meanness from your life. You have enough to deal with right now.

## EMPOWERED PARENTING AFFIRMATIONS

I will not accept undue judgment of myself as a parent.

I will not accept undue judgment of my child or my family.

I will not allow others' judgments to bring me down.

## SELF-REFLECTION

Make a list of the people in your life who are the most judgmental.

_____

_____

_____

_____

Make a list of the people in your life who are the least judgmental.

_____

_____

_____

_____

Which list is longer? Write about why you think that is and what you can do to ensure that you're better supported during difficult times.

Finish the following sentences and free-write for a few minutes on each:

When I am judged as a parent _____

When others judge my child _____

When others judge my journey _____

I can counteract judgment by _____

_____
_____
_____
_____
_____
_____
_____
_____
_____
_____

## SURROUND YOURSELF WITH SUPPORTIVE FRIENDS AND FAMILY

Just as Shelley helped me go through the house to make sure Noel would be safe when she came home, many other friends and family members supported us along the way.

My friends Debbie and Karen (and Karen's entire family) helped us pack our belongings as the girls and I moved to our new home. Their friendship helped us through the overwhelming transition.

> Their friendship helped us through the overwhelming transition.

My brother Rick came for two weeks and ticked off the to-do list of needed repairs in the house, helping me create a comfortable haven for myself and my girls. My sister-in-law Nancy helped me paint the deck while I cried and shared my daunting feeling of utter aloneness as a single parent dealing with so much.

After Noel's first suicide attempt, I made countless calls to my friends Jamie and Lucy and my sister Gail. They counseled and soothed. They were there to listen when I needed to share.

My friend Sandra brought me lovely flowers and sat in the garden with me as I sobbed, surrounding me with her kindness and love.

My neighbor Stephanie was there for us the whole time, loving and supporting our family without judgment, always there when we needed something.

Her home became a safe place for my children to run to in emergencies, and she kept a watchful eye over their comings and goings.

My boyfriend John entered my life right around that time too. What terrible timing to start a romance! I certainly wasn't looking for it, but I know he came into my life then for a reason. He helped me talk through the ordeals I was facing. He was rock solid in his support, advice, and encouragement.

My family wouldn't have been able to make it through without these people and many other wonderful friends and family members who supported us throughout our trials. These angels lifted us up in our darkest moments.

**Find the people who support you. Find the people who make you laugh, who are there for you, and who don't judge you. Find the ones who feed your weary soul.**

## EMPOWERED PARENTING AFFIRMATION

I will actively seek to surround myself with people who support my family's emotional wellness and healing.

## SELF-REFLECTION

Make a list of ways that others have supported you.

_____
_____
_____
_____
_____

Write about how this support helps you and makes you feel.

_____
_____
_____
_____
_____

Make a list of what you still need help with.

_____

_____

_____

_____

_____

_____

_____

Make a list of all the people or resources you could reach out to, to ask for this help.

_____

_____

_____

_____

_____

_____

_____

_____

## KEEP A THICK SKIN

Being the safe person for your suicidal child—the one they turn to in their darkest moments—also means you may become the punching bag as they unleash their agony on you. They may even blame you for where they've landed in life.

"It's all your fault, Mom! You're a bad parent!"

Or, "I hate you, Dad!"

> Stay compassionate, and don't take it personally.

Be prepared. You may be sworn at, lied to, deceived, guilt-tripped. Your child may hurl insults, convey a bad attitude, or yell at you—sometimes when you're out in public.

Your child knows you're terrified right now. They may try to use your fear against you, saying things like, "If you ground me for smoking pot, I swear I'm going to kill myself!"

I was horrified and bewildered to find my innocent children replaced by these angry strangers. Where did my kids go?

It hurts to be lashed out at as a parent . . . but it hurts even more to see your child in pain.

Stay compassionate, and don't take it personally. They're suffering, and the process of working through that can be ugly and painful. They aren't themselves right now.

Speak up and demand respect. Even though your child is hurting, you can't just step back and let them railroad you. It's a delicate balance to know when to call out the behavior and when to let it go, but hold your children accountable for their poor choices or actions.

Be patient. Admittedly, this is difficult when your life becomes a living hell. However, this type of change is gradual, and it takes time. You're in it for the long haul; there are no shortcuts or quick fixes. You, as a parent, will need to persevere.

All of this takes a giant leap of faith that your child can be well, that normalcy can be attained again. But I'm here to tell you that there is hope on the other side.

## EMPOWERED PARENTING AFFIRMATIONS

I am worthy of respect and love—no matter what.

I will stay strong when I'm affected by my child's decision to lash out.

## SELF-REFLECTION

Fill in the blanks below. Elaborate on your responses by free-writing about each sentence for a few minutes.

When my child _____ ,

I feel _____

_____

_____

_____

When my child _____ ,

I feel _____

_____

_____

_____

_____

When my child _____ ,

I feel _____

_____

_____

_____

Write how you respond when your child lashes out. Is there a better way to react?

## TAKE IT DAY BY DAY

Treatment for mental illness doesn't bring overnight results. Addressing these issues may take months, even years. It can be a long road.

Medications can help smooth out the edges and tame extreme mood swings. They may be needed for short-term stabilization or be prescribed for longer periods of time. It can take some trial and error to find the correct medication or dosage.

> Don't look too far into the future right now. Instead, stay grounded in the reality of today and take each moment as it comes. Deal with one thing at a time.

Therapy can help immensely, but it usually takes a series of sessions to see results. A certain therapist may not gel with your child, and you may need to try another whose personality or techniques bring better results. All of this also takes time.

I know this isn't very encouraging—especially if you're sleeping on the floor outside your child's bedroom every night to make sure nothing happens. It's hard to think of this going on for a long time. It's incredibly disheartening.

Don't look too far into the future right now. Instead, stay grounded in the reality of today and take each moment as it comes. Deal with one thing at a time.

You've been holding your breath for a while now, I know. Take a deep breath. Then another. You can do this.

## EMPOWERED PARENTING AFFIRMATION

I will stay the course for as long as it takes to achieve healing for myself and my family.

## SELF-REFLECTION

Complete the following sentences:

I feel strong when _____

_____

_____

_____

I feel stronger when _____

_____

_____

_____

I feel strongest when _____

_____

_____

_____

What are your sources of strength? What helps you keep going?

## BE GENTLE WITH YOURSELF

If I've learned anything on this journey, it's how easy it is to blame myself as a parent. The voices of doubt used to play over and over in my mind:

"Wow, I'm so stupid. How could I not have seen this?"

"I'm a lousy parent. I did everything wrong."

"I should've left him sooner."

"How did I lose control over this?"

"I should've done more."

"I should've seen the signs."

> Be gentle with yourself. No matter what, you can only do so much. Even a gold-star parent is going to make mistakes. You're human. No one is perfect.

On and on it went with the blame. I could practically look over my shoulder and see myself back there with the whip: "It's all your fault! Try harder!"

Be gentle with yourself. No matter what, you can only do so much. Even a gold-star parent is going to make mistakes. You're human. No one is perfect.

No matter how hard you try, parenting a depressed or suicidal child is difficult. You'll lose your patience in these stressful times, and you may act in ways you would've never dreamed. Your parenting skills will be tested.

Let go of the past and what you can't change. Forgive yourself. Forgive your ex. Forgive your child. Acceptance will help you move forward and take the necessary steps to healing.

## EMPOWERED PARENTING AFFIRMATIONS

I give myself grace for my mistakes.

I am enough.

I've done the best I can.

## SELF-REFLECTION

Make a list of all the negative voices that play in your head. What are they saying? Write each as a statement. For each negative statement, write an opposing statement that counteracts it and is positive and affirming to you.

My negative thought: _____

_____

_____

_____

My positive counter-response: _____

_____

_____

_____

_____

My negative thought: _____

_____

_____

_____

My positive counter-response: _____

_____

_____

_____

My negative thought: _____

_____

_____

_____

My positive counter-response: _____

_____

_____

_____

## 10

## GET REAL ABOUT YOUR OWN ISSUES

Yes, you need to give yourself grace as a parent, but it's also time to look in the mirror and be honest with yourself.

Do you have things you need to work on? Do you drink a lot or have other substance abuse issues? Do you have mental health challenges? Do you have an anger problem?

Are some of your behaviors contributing to the current issues and adding stress?

> Your support is critical, and you need to be emotionally well to face this. Now is the time for you to rise. Your child needs you to be your best self.

Would getting professional help allow you to parent from a healthier space? Would it help your family be healthier and more resilient? Would you feel better? Would it help you to better deal with the situation at hand? Above all, would it help you be a better parent?

If you answered "yes" to any of these questions, it's time to help yourself. It will take you a step closer to being the supportive parent you want to be.

When your child feels suicidal, they need you more than ever before. Your support is critical, and you need to be emotionally well to face this. Now is the time for you to rise. Your child needs you to be your best self.

## EMPOWERED PARENTING AFFIRMATIONS

I will stay honest with myself about my own state of mind.

I will do everything possible to function as the best parent I can be.

## SELF-REFLECTION

Write about how you feel about yourself as a parent. Are you approaching situations in the best way?

Are you emotionally healthy? Do you need to find help for anything you're struggling with?

## 11

## STAY POSITIVE

Despite the daunting circumstances, you need to do everything in your power to maintain a positive mindset.

When crisis strikes, it isn't the time for anger or blame. You have to deal with what's in front of you before you can deal with the factors that contributed to the situation.

> If you stay calm and positive, remembering that your child is acting from a place of pain, you can get through the moment in a more productive way.

You may be exasperated by the poor choices your child is making. But if you stay calm and positive, remembering that your child is acting from a place of pain, you can get through the moment in a more productive way.

When my girls began to deal with depression and suicidal thoughts, I faced my own pain, grief, fear, and overwhelm. But I refused to give up the vision that we would one day heal.

I tried not to have a "poor me" or "poor us" attitude. Once you start to feel sorry for yourself, it's a downward slide. Gratitude creates powerful energy that can shift everything around you.

I trained myself to see the silver linings, to grasp at the moments of joy that threaded their way into the tapestry of our trials. If all you ever do is focus on the negative, your memories will remain negative.

Where are the bits of joy in your life right now? Work to find them, and practice noticing them and feeling thankful for them whenever they arrive.

Celebrate all the wins you possibly can. Is this the first day in a while that your depressed teen got out of bed? That's a win. Did your child react calmly to a stressful situation instead of acting out? That's a win.

Few things change overnight. Move forward toward healing and embrace each positive step as it happens. You'll find things to celebrate once you change your mindset to look for them.

Do your research, and get your hands on all the information you can. Read books and articles, peruse websites, take online classes, watch videos, listen to podcasts . . . do all you can to learn what's going on with your child. Listen to the advice of others who are experts in the field or who have walked this path as a fellow parent.

Don't give up! As a family, we tackled each problem as it surfaced. We tried things, and if they didn't work, we tried something else.

Dig down, deep inside yourself, to find the strength to keep going. It's a terrible situation. Do all you can, of course, but also know that it's not all in your hands. Control what you can . . . and pray for the rest.

Above all else, as a family, treat each other kindly. Treat yourself kindly too.

When people ask me how we got through this as a family, and how I endured it as a parent, I simply tell them that we kept the faith. We never let go of hope because it's what got us through from one day to the next. Hope is the most powerful force of all.

# EMPOWERED PARENTING AFFIRMATION

I will do everything I can to remain positive and hopeful.

## SELF-REFLECTION

Do you feel that you approach crises positively or negatively? How so?

_____
_____
_____
_____

Make a list of all the negative things happening in your life right now. Don't hold back—write as many as you can.

_____
_____
_____
_____
_____
_____

For everything on your list, find three (or more!) things for which you can be grateful in that situation. Where are the silver linings?

Make a list of ways you can stay positive.

## 12

## STAY TRUE TO UNCONDITIONAL LOVE

Starting when she was around eighteen months old, Jane had severe tantrums four or five times a day. Sometimes she would scream and cry for thirty minutes straight. She would thrash violently and sometimes even froth at the mouth.

She was my firstborn, so I wasn't sure if this should be happening or if I was doing something wrong. I finally called the doctor, who told me it was normal for children her age.

> "When she feels out of control of her emotions, what do you think she needs from you in that moment?"

But I found myself getting worked up alongside her. She would throw a tantrum; I would get upset.

Thankfully, I received great advice from a therapist who asked me, "When she feels out of control of her emotions, what do you think she needs from you in that moment?"

"Reassurance," I responded. "Love."

"Exactly."

This changed the trajectory of my parenting, as I rejected the then-popular notion that time-outs were the solution to tantrums. While I'd used them at first, time-outs had never felt right to me. It seemed like punishing Jane for simply having emotions that didn't fit into "acceptable" behavior.

I changed my approach. When she would scream and cry, I would hold out my arms to her and ask, "What do you need from Mama right now? Do you need me to hold you?"

She almost always accepted the loving invitation to connect—a far cry from the punitive approach I'd used before. It created trust, and the tantrums subsided.

> When we create a bond of trust in the early years, we establish a relationship that can withstand other stressors in the years to come.

When we create a bond of trust in the early years, we establish a relationship that can withstand other stressors in the years to come.

The phrase "unconditional love" means we accept our child no matter what. When you have a child who's thriving and excelling, it's easy to say, "I love my child unconditionally." It brings forward happy, proud feelings of love.

When your child swears at you, lies to you, does drugs, slaps you in the face, screams at you, or makes poor decision after poor decision… that's when you need to dig deep for that unconditional love.

Maybe depression has hijacked your once-cheerful, easygoing child. Maybe you're tired of their sullenness or lack of cooperation. Maybe you're disappointed or scared for them (or even scared *of* them). Maybe you're frustrated and angry.

You don't understand why they make the choices they do. You don't understand why they want to die. You just know it hurts so much to see them suffering.

Saying "I love my child unconditionally" feels a little different now, doesn't it? It's not a rosy, warm feeling this time. Now, "unconditional" love takes a different form. It's raw, it's real, and it's tested. It's hard. Now, there's a feeling of perseverance, of defiance.

Your love endures despite the difficulties. Your love is fierce.

You love this child. No matter what. This child means everything to you.

You know the meaning of unconditional love because every day, despite your fear and despair, you battle on.

You are essential in your child's journey to emotional wellness. Your unconditional love will support them as they move through it.

Love creates the hope that keeps you going. You can't give up; your child desperately needs you. You can and will overcome anything if you stay positive, proactive, and strong.

## EMPOWERED PARENTING AFFIRMATIONS

Despite my fears, disappointments, and pain, I will stay true to unconditional love.

My child is worthy of my love—no matter what.

I will never give up.

## SELF-REFLECTION

During this time, what has been your greatest disappointment?

What hurts you the most right now?

_____
_____
_____
_____
_____
_____
_____

What worries you the most? What are you most afraid of?

_____
_____
_____
_____
_____
_____
_____

What can you do to be proactive in getting your child to the point of healing?

What brings you hope?

What brings you joy?

_____
_____
_____
_____
_____
_____
_____
_____
_____

What will you always love about your child?

_____
_____
_____
_____
_____
_____
_____
_____
_____

What are you grateful for?

How will you persevere as a family?

What lessons have come to you in this journey?

What are your hopes and dreams for the future of your child and your family?

What proactive steps can you take so your child, your family, and you can achieve healing?

# 12 WAYS
# TO EMPOWER
# YOUR PARENTING

A REFERENCE GUIDE

## 12 WAYS TO EMPOWER YOUR PARENTING

# FIND OUTSIDE SUPPORT

**EMPOWERED PARENTING AFFIRMATION**

I'm not alone in facing this. I can reach out to others who are willing to help.

# 12 WAYS TO EMPOWER YOUR PARENTING

## LET IT GO

**EMPOWERED PARENTING AFFIRMATION**

I allow myself to release what weighs me down.

## 12 WAYS TO EMPOWER YOUR PARENTING

# REDUCE SCREEN TIME

**EMPOWERED PARENTING AFFIRMATION**

I will stay open to the awareness of what outside influences are affecting my children and my family.

# 12 WAYS TO EMPOWER YOUR PARENTING

## TAKE CARE OF YOURSELF

**EMPOWERED PARENTING AFFIRMATION**

I am worthy of love and self-care. Taking care of myself will make me stronger and better able to help my family.

# 12 WAYS TO EMPOWER YOUR PARENTING

# AVOID UNSYMPATHETIC JUDGERS

**EMPOWERED PARENTING AFFIRMATIONS**

I will not accept undue judgment of myself as a parent.

I will not accept undue judgment of my child or my family.

I will not allow others' judgments to bring me down.

# 12 WAYS TO EMPOWER YOUR PARENTING

# SURROUND YOURSELF WITH SUPPORTIVE FRIENDS AND FAMILY

**EMPOWERED PARENTING AFFIRMATION**

I will actively seek to surround myself with people who support my family's emotional wellness and healing.

# 12 WAYS TO EMPOWER YOUR PARENTING

## KEEP A THICK SKIN

**EMPOWERED PARENTING AFFIRMATIONS**

I am worthy of respect and love—no matter what.

I will stay strong when I'm affected by my child's decision to lash out.

# 12 WAYS TO EMPOWER YOUR PARENTING

# TAKE IT DAY BY DAY

**EMPOWERED PARENTING AFFIRMATION**

I will stay the course for as long as it takes to achieve healing for myself and my family.

## 12 WAYS TO EMPOWER YOUR PARENTING

# BE GENTLE WITH YOURSELF

**EMPOWERED PARENTING AFFIRMATIONS**

I give myself grace for my mistakes.

I am enough.

I've done the best I can.

## 12 WAYS TO EMPOWER YOUR PARENTING

# GET REAL ABOUT YOUR OWN ISSUES

**EMPOWERED PARENTING AFFIRMATIONS**

I will stay honest with myself about my own state of mind.

I will do everything possible to function as the best parent I can be.

# 12 WAYS TO EMPOWER YOUR PARENTING

## STAY POSITIVE

**EMPOWERED PARENTING AFFIRMATION**

I will do everything I can to remain positive and hopeful.

## 12 WAYS TO EMPOWER YOUR PARENTING

# STAY TRUE TO UNCONDITIONAL LOVE

**EMPOWERED PARENTING AFFIRMATIONS**

Despite my fears, disappointments, and pain, I will stay true to unconditional love.

My child is worthy of my love— no matter what.

I will never give up.

# Part Four

HELPFUL RESOURCES

## PODCAST

My family's pain has turned into a mission to help others. I've created a podcast, *Empowered Parenting for Emotional Wellness*, in which I interview mental health experts and advocates to learn ways to strengthen emotional resilience in our children, tweens, and teens. A Pinterest board of additional resources accompanies each episode.

Through education and awareness, we can empower ourselves to be the best parents we can be.

**Learn more at hopefuldawn.com/podcast.**

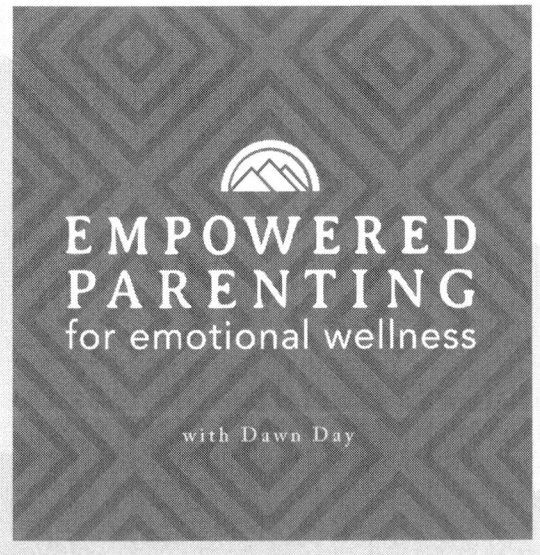

# BOOKS

Here are some of the books that helped me and my girls understand what we were going through and make positive changes.

## BOOKS FOR ADULTS

*Adolescent Depression: A Guide for Parents* by Francis Mark Mondimore, MD, and Patrick Kelly, MD

*Helping Your Anxious Teen: Positive Parenting Strategies to Help Your Teen Beat Anxiety, Stress and Worry* by Sheila Achar Josephs

*If Your Adolescent Has Depression or Bipolar Disorder: An Essential Resource for Parents* by Dwight L. Evans, MD, and Linda Wasmer Andrews

*Parenting a Teen Who Has Intense Emotions: DBT Skills to Help Your Teen Navigate Emotional and Behavioral Challenges* by Pat Harvey and Britt H. Rathbone

*Parenting the New Teen in the Age of Anxiety: A Complete Guide to Your Child's Stressed, Depressed, Expanded, Amazing Adolescence* by Dr. John Duffy

*Rescuing Your Teenager from Depression* by Norman T. Berlinger, MD

*Understanding Teenage Anxiety: A Parent's Guide to Improving Your Teen's Mental Health* by Jennifer Browne and Cody Buchanan

*Untangled: Guiding Teenage Girls Through the Seven Transitions into Adulthood* by Lisa Damour, PhD

## BOOKS FOR CHILDREN, TWEENS, AND TEENS

*Anger Management Workbook for Kids: 50 Fun Activities to Help Children Stay Calm and Make Better Choices When They Feel Mad* by Samantha Snowden, MA

*Anxiety Relief for Teens: Essential CBT Skills and Self-Care Practices to Overcome Anxiety and Stress* by Regine Galanti

*Conquer Negative Thinking for Teens: A Workbook to Break the Nine Thought Habits That Are Holding You Back* by Mary Karapetian Alvord and Anne McGrath

*Depression: A Teen's Guide to Survive and Thrive* by Jacqueline B. Toner and Claire A. B. Freeland

*It's Your Weirdness That Makes You Wonderful: A Self-Acceptance Prompt Journal* by Kate Allan

*The Depression Workbook for Teens: Tools to Improve Your Mood, Build Self-Esteem, and Stay Motivated* by Katie Hurley, LCSW

*The Ultimate Self-Esteem Workbook for Teens: Overcome Insecurity, Defeat Your Inner Critic, and Live Confidently* by Megan MacCutcheon, LPC

*Understanding Suicide: A National Epidemic* by Connie Goldsmith

*When Nothing Matters Anymore: A Survival Guide for Depressed Teens* by Bev Cobain, RNC, and Elizabeth Verdick

*You're Strong, Smart, and You Got This: Drawings, Affirmations, and Comfort to Help with Anxiety and Depression* by Kate Allan

# ORGANIZATIONS

Here is a list of organizations that may be able to help you and your family. Please note that this isn't an endorsement of any programs or services in particular, and keep in mind that these details may change at any time.

## SUICIDE PREVENTION

**National Suicide Prevention Lifeline**
1-800-273-TALK

**National Hopeline Network**
1-800-SUICIDE

**American Association of Suicidology (AAS)**
5221 Wisconsin Avenue, NW, 2nd Floor, Washington, DC 20015
suicidology.org

With a goal of reducing suicide nationwide, AAS partners with mental health professionals, school districts, and survivors of suicide loss. AAS supports suicide prevention, intervention, and postvention.

**American Foundation for Suicide Prevention (AFSP)**
199 Water Street, 11th Floor, New York, NY 10038
afsp.org

AFSP provides support programs for those struggling with mental illness, as well as those who've lost a loved one to suicide. If you or someone you know is in crisis, keep their number handy: 800-273-8255.

*...continued on next page*

**American Psychiatric Association (APA)**
800 Maine Ave. SW, Washington, DC 20024
psych.org

With suicide rates increasing in almost every state, the APA stands prepared to deal with the crisis through a network of nearly 40,000 psychiatrists. APA is the voice and conscience of modern psychiatry.

**American Psychological Association (APA)**
750 First Street, NE, Washington, DC 20002-4242
apa.org

The APA is the largest professional organization of psychologists in the US with over 120,000 members. As suicide increases in people aged fifteen to twenty-four, APA psychologists help parents like you recognize the warning signs, then take steps to prevent it.

**Brain Injury Association of America (BIAA)**
3057 Nutley Street #805, Fairfax, VA 22031
biausa.org

Suicide risk is higher in people with traumatic brain injury—in fact, the risk triples in the first six months following that injury. What's more, brain injury is often a misdiagnosed and misunderstood neurological disease. As the nation's oldest and largest brain injury organization, the BIAA offers care and support for those with brain injury and their families.

**Canadian Association for Suicide Prevention (CASP)**
P.O. Box 53082, RPO Rideau Centre, Ottawa, ON K1N 1C5 Canada
suicideprevention.ca

Whether you're having thoughts of suicide or you're a suicide survivor, CASP is there with intervention, postvention, and life promotion within Canada. The association envisions a Canada without suicide by working with communities to reduce the suicide rate and minimize the harmful consequences of suicidal behavior.

## Centre for Suicide Prevention (CSP)
105 12th Avenue SE, Suite 320, Calgary, AB T2G 1A1 Canada
suicideinfo.ca

CSP is a Canadian education center with a library of over 45,000 suicide-specific items—the largest English-language collection of its kind. CSP educates online, in print, and interactively. They can help you develop the knowledge and skills necessary to help those at high risk of suicide.

## Depression and Bipolar Support Alliance (DBSA)
55 E Jackson Blvd., Suite 490, Chicago, IL 60604
dbsalliance.org

Mood disorders affect over 21 million Americans and account for more than 50 percent of the nation's suicides every year. DBSA provides hope, help, support, and education to those with depression and bipolar disorder. With six hundred support groups and more than two hundred chapters nationwide, DBSA offers in-person and online peer support if you or someone you love suffers from mental illness or is thinking of suicide.

## Harvard School of Public Health (HSPH)
hsph.harvard.edu

HSPH is the public health school of Harvard University. With a mission to improve the lives and health of people everywhere, HSPH developed the "Means Matter" campaign to assess whether a person at risk for suicide has access to a firearm or lethal means, then work with their family to limit their access until they're no longer at elevated risk.

## International Foundation for Research and Education on Depression (iFred)
P.O. Box 17598, Baltimore, MD 21297-1598
ifred.org

Research consistently shows a strong link between suicide and depression. iFred is one of the few organizations researching the causes of depression while also helping those coping with depression and suicidal ideation on an international scale. Its goal is to ensure that 100 percent of the 350 million people affected by depression seek help and treatment.

**Jason Foundation**
18 Volunteer Drive, Hendersonville, TN 37075
jasonfoundation.com

We lose an average of 130 young people each week to suicide. The Jason Foundation is dedicated to educating students, teachers, and community organizations about the risk and prevention of teen suicide. It operates a crisis hotline, 1-800-273-8255, as well as educational curriculum promoting teen-suicide awareness.

**The Jed Foundation**
P.O. Box 60174, Brooklyn, NY 11206
jedfoundation.org
ulifeline.org

Suicide is currently the second-most common cause of death among college students. The Jed Foundation is dedicated to raising awareness of suicide deaths on US college campuses while establishing connections between academic communities and higher-education professionals who work directly with college students. The foundation also developed ulifeline.org, an online resource for college students struggling with depression and stress.

**National Alliance on Mental Illness (NAMI)**
4301 Wilson Blvd., Suite 300, Arlington, VA 22203
nami.org

NAMI is the nation's largest grassroots mental health organization and the leading voice on mental health. The alliance is dedicated to building better lives for the millions of Americans affected by mental illness. NAMI is a consumer advocacy and support organization composed largely of family members of those suffering from severe mental illnesses. If you're in crisis or know someone who is, call 800-950-6264.

## Samaritans USA

samaritansusa.org

Samaritans is the world's oldest and largest suicide-prevention network, with four hundred centers in thirty-eight countries. Through multiple branches in the US, Samaritans USA provides confidential counseling and other assistance to those who are struggling to cope or are worried about someone else.

## Society for the Prevention of Teen Suicide (SPTS)

110 W. Main Street, Freehold, NJ 07728

sptsusa.org

With a mission of reducing youth suicides and attempted suicides, SPTS has developed training programs for teens, parents, and educators. Their website offers educators a two-hour suicide awareness training program and a suicide-prevention hotline: 800-273-8255.

## Suicide Awareness Voices of Education (SAVE)

7900 Xerxes Avenue South, Suite 810, Bloomington, MN 55431

save.org

SAVE's members believe that brain diseases such as depression should be detected and treated promptly to help prevent suicide. To that end, SAVE works to prevent suicide and help those grieving following the loss of a loved one. Additionally, they provide the tools community leaders need to help prevent suicide.

# BULLYING

## Champions Against Bullying (CAB)
650 Poydras Street, Suite 1470, New Orleans, LA 70130
championsagainstbullying.org

CAB is a nonprofit fighting bullying, in part, by partnering with actors and writers to spread the message that bullying is real and can be stopped. These "star champions" visit schools and speak with kids about the impact bullying can have. The organization provides science-backed anti-bullying resources.

## Generations Against Bullying (GAB)
6550 West Forest Home Avenue, Milwaukee, WI 53220
gabnow.org

GAB provides a proven anti-bullying solution for schools that encourages students to step in and act when they witness a classmate being victimized. GAB's Peer Ambassador Upstander Programs work with, train, and encourage schools and students to reduce episodes of bullying through a non-threatening approach that shifts the culture of bullying into a culture of love, acceptance, and encouragement.

## Kind Campaign
Malibu, CA
kindcampaign.com

Kind Campaign is an internationally recognized nonprofit that brings awareness and healing to the negative and lasting effects of girl-against-girl bullying through documentary films, in-school assemblies, international school tours, and educational curriculums. Kind Campaign's website is a robust resource, helping girls learn about the impact of bullying on others and themselves.

## PACER's National Bullying Prevention Center
8161 Normandale Blvd., Bloomington, MN 55437

pacer.org/bullying

PACER actively leads social change to prevent childhood bullying so that all youth are safe and supported in their schools, communities, and online. The center also provides crucial resources for students, parents, and educators while recognizing bullying as a serious community issue that impacts education, physical and emotional health, and the safety and well-being of students.

## National Association of People Against Bullying (NAPAB)
2854 Calle Esteban, San Clemente, CA 92673

napab.org

NAPAB is a nonprofit foundation providing anti-bullying services, education, advocacy, and support to students, families, and school administrators. With a goal of promoting a harassment-free society, schools form student-run anti-bullying Cool 2 Be Kind chapters to combat bullying. Additionally, NAPAB provides victims of bullying with therapy, martial arts, and private investigative services.

## No Bully
1012 Torney Avenue, San Francisco, CA 94129

nobully.org

No Bully's mission is to eradicate bullying and cyberbullying worldwide. The organization's unique "No Bully System" guides K–12 teachers through interventions designed to end bullying. Teachers are trained to identify, interrupt, and intervene when bullying occurs. A written anti-bullying protocol and action steps support and sustain an inclusive school culture while igniting compassion in the next generation.

### Stand for the Silent (SFTS)
6918 West 128th Street, Perkins, OK, 74059
standforthesilent.org

With 1,620,000 kids reached in over 1,500 schools, SFTS brings awareness to bullying and the devastation it causes. The nonprofit encourages building a SFTS chapter of students who are committed to change and will not stand for their peers to suffer at the hands of a bully. The organization also provides celebrity endorsement videos.

### STOMP Out Bullying
220 East 57th Street, Suite G, New York, NY 10022-2820
stompoutbullying.org

STOMP Out Bullying works to reduce and prevent bullying and cyberbullying while educating against homophobia, LGBTQ discrimination, racism, and hatred. With a goal of "ending the hate and changing the culture," the organization works to deter violence in schools, online, and in communities across the country. It also helps those in need and at risk of suicide through peer-mentoring programs in schools.

### Stop Bullying
U.S. Department of Health and Human Services
200 Independence Ave. SW, Washington, DC 20201
stopbullying.gov

This government organization provides information on what bullying is, who is at risk, and how kids, teens, young adults, parents, educators, and others in the community can prevent or stop bullying. The organization helps communities develop a bullying-prevention strategy by providing free fact sheets, research summaries, and intervention strategies.

# PHYSICAL, SEXUAL & EMOTIONAL ABUSE

**American Professional Society on the Abuse of Children (APSAC)**
590 Avenue of the Americas, 14th Floor, New York, NY 10011
apsac.org

APSAC addresses all facets of the professional response to child maltreatment: prevention, assessment, intervention, and treatment. With the goal of preventing and eliminating the recurrence of child maltreatment, APSAC connects professionals to cases while educating the public about abuse and neglect.

**American Psychological Association**
750 First Street, NE, Washington, DC 20002
apa.org

The APA is the largest scientific and professional organization representing psychology in the country. The APA Violence Prevention Office (VPO) focuses on violence and injury prevention, as well as topics associated with child maltreatment, trauma, media violence, and youth violence. The association recognizes the contributions of psychologists to the prevention of violence.

**Center for Violence and Injury Prevention**
1 Brookings Drive, Campus Box 1196, St. Louis, MO 63130
cvip.wustl.edu

With a mission of promoting healthy young families and young adults, the Center for Violence and Injury Prevention provides evidence-based violence prevention through education, research, and training activities. In doing so, they help put an end to child abuse, sexual violence, suicide, and intimate-partner violence.

**Children's Safety Network (CSN)**
43 Foundry Avenue, Waltham, MA 02453-8313
childrenssafetynetwork.org

CSN works with maternal and child health, as well as injury- and violence-prevention programs to create an environment in which all infants, children, and youth are safe and healthy. CSN's goal is to equip states to strengthen their capacity, utilize data, and implement strategies to prevent injury-related deaths, hospitalizations, and emergency visits.

**Child Molestation Research & Prevention Institute**
1151 Harbor Bay Parkway, Suite 121, Alameda, CA 94502
childmolestationprevention.org

The Child Molestation Research & Prevention Institute is a national, science-based organization dedicated to preventing child sexual abuse through research, education, and family support. The institute disseminates information to professionals and families about the warning signs of abuse as well as early diagnosis and treatment.

**ChildHelp**
6730 N. Scottsdale Road, Suite 150, Scottsdale, AZ 85253
childhelp.org

ChildHelp's approach to childhood abuse and neglect focuses on prevention, intervention, and treatment. The ChildHelp National Child Abuse Hotline, 1-800-4-A-CHILD, operates 24/7, 365 days a year, and the organization's programs and services include residential treatment services; children's advocacy centers; child abuse prevention, education, and training; and the National Day of Hope.

### Child Welfare League of America (CWLA)
727 15th Street NW, Suite 1200, Washington, DC 20005
cwla.org

CWLA is the oldest national organization serving vulnerable children, youth, and their families. CWLA provides training, consultation, and technical assistance to child welfare professionals and agencies on emerging issues affecting abused, neglected, and at-risk children. Publications, conferences, and teleconferences are also available.

### Coalition for Children
P.O. Box 6304, Denver, CO 80206
safechild.org

The Coalition for Children offers the Safe Child Program, a preschool-through-eighth-grade curriculum that teaches the prevention of sexual, emotional, and physical abuse by persons known to the child; the prevention of abuse and abduction; and safety in self-care.

### Prevent Child Abuse America (PCAA)
228 South Wabash Avenue, 10th Floor, Chicago, IL 60604
preventchildabuse.org

PCAA promotes legislation, policies, and programs that help prevent child abuse and neglect, support healthy childhood development, and strengthen families. Working in partnership with the National Center on Child Abuse Prevention Research and Resources, PCAA develops prevention strategies and disseminates information about child abuse across the country.

### Stop It Now!
351 Pleasant Street, Suite B-319, Northampton, MA 01060
stopitnow.org

Stop It Now! prevents the sexual abuse of children by mobilizing adults, families, and communities to take action before a child is harmed. The organization offers a helpline, 1-888-PREVENT, an online help center, and an "Ask Now" advice column.

*If you enjoyed this book, would you consider leaving a review? Even just a few words will help others decide if the book is right for them.*

*It's quick and easy. Navigate to the book's page on Amazon, and scroll down to the Customer Reviews section of the page, just underneath the author's bio. There's a button there that says "Write a Customer Review." Click that to be taken to the "Your Reviews" page.*

*If you know others who can benefit from this book, please let them know! Go to hopefuldawn.com/book and use the share buttons to individually email the link or to share to your social media.*

*Thank you for reading!*

Made in the USA
Middletown, DE
07 October 2021